Application Program Generators

A State of the Art Survey

R F Lobell

PUBLISHED BY NCC PUBLICATIONS

87 — 0617450
(AWMXE)

British Library Cataloguing in Publication Data

Lobell, R. F.
  Application program generators.
  1. Computer programs
  I. Title
  001.64'25   QA76.7

ISBN 0-85012-412-3

First published in 1983 by:

NCC Publications, The National Computing Centre Limited, Oxford Road, Manchester M1 7ED, England.

Typeset in 10pt Times Roman by UPS Blackburn Ltd, 76-80 Northgate, Blackburn, Lancashire and printed by Hobbs the Printers of Southampton.

ISBN 0-85012-412-3

Contents

1 Background and Historical Context

Considering its size and importance, computing is a relatively young industry. It is, in fact, barely 30 years old and yet in this period there have already been several 'generations' of computing.

The first generation is generally accepted as having begun in the early 1950s when the first computing machines became commercially available. Until then, computing had been confined to university laboratories and the 'programmers' were the scientists and engineers working on the development of these early stored-program machines.

The university prototypes, such as the Manchester University Mark 1 (probably the world's first programmable computer), were programmed in a primitive machine code and had very limited storage and input-output facilities.

Early programs were usually 'number crunching' mathematical routines designed to exercise the computer's logic or were one-off solutions to problems which could not be solved by manual methods. The computer was used purely for executing machine code instructions which acted directly on the hardware. Support for program development was minimal and a great deal of manual effort was required to produce even small programs.

The generalised use of computing meant that computers were going to be used by people who were interested not in the computer itself but in its use as a tool for solving particular problems. The new users were not intimately involved in computer design and development, but were interested in using the arithmetic power of the computer to solve their own problems in other branches of science, engineering and, later, commerce. The requirements of these new users led to the development of a second generation of computing, incorporating symbolic languages which effectively shielded the user from the hardware architecture of the machine. The symbolic language provided a more meaningful mnemonic notation for users, allowing them to concentrate more on the problem to be solved rather than the process going on within the computer. Along with the first symbolic languages appeared rudimentary monitors providing a limited amount of programming support for the user. The monitors included primitive debugging facilities for examining the contents of registers and single stepping through a computation.

By the late 1950s, however, it became clear that symbolic languages and rudimentary monitors were not sufficient to support the growing number of prospective users of computing. The scientific and engineering community, being still considered to be the primary users of computers, were the first to benefit with, initially, the development of an Autocode compiler in the UK (Mark 1 Autocode for the Ferranti Star range 1954), followed by the arrival of the first widely recognised high-level language, FORTRAN, in 1957.

The use of such high-level languages was the precursor to the third generation of computing.

The idea of a high-level language was to provide the users with a syntax which describes the sorts of operations they would be most likely to require in order to solve their problems. FORTRAN (FORmula TRANslation language) attempted to describe mathematical, scientific and engineering calculations in a way which was readily understandable to those requiring the results of these calculations.

The users would, in theory, need to have no knowledge of the internal operations of the computer which executed the program. The language also incorporated all the input and output handling experiments of the application.

Languages like FORTRAN require a compiler to be resident in the machine's main memory to translate the high-level source code written by the user into the low-level object code which the machine would actually execute.

Early FORTRAN compilers concentrated on optimisation of the object code, within the severe space and time constraints imposed by the computer hardware technology of the time, at the expense of translation efficiency. At the time this was thought to be acceptable since a program would be compiled once and then be executed in its object code form many times. An example of the translation inefficiency is provided by the fact that the IBM 704 FORTRAN 1 compiler took approximately one minute to translate a program consisting of the simple statement STOP.

Despite their shortcomings, however, high-level languages like FORTRAN (designed for the scientific community) and the COmmon Business Oriented Language, COBOL (designed for the rapidly growing commercial data processing community and first introduced in 1961) were a giant step forward in applications software.

Throughout the 1960s computers continued to be improved and more hardware and software services became available. The cost of the hardware fell rapidly whilst, at the same time, spectacular advances were being made in hardware fabrication technology. Thermionic devices had already been displaced by transistors in the processing circuits, leading to reductions in size, power consumption and cost and an increase in circuit reliability. Similar advances were made in storage technology, with Williams Tubes and magnetic drums giving way to magnetic core, tape and disks. Storage capacities increased whilst the cost of that capacity fell. Improved input and output devices, such as high-speed card reader/punches and fast printers, superseded slower paper tape reader/punches and teletype printers.

The introduction of integrated circuits in the mid-1960s further drove down the cost, size and power consumption of computer hardware whilst continuing to improve the reliability of the processing circuits. The falling cost of the hardware provided the impetus for the increased use of computers and throughout the 1960s and early 1970s there was a massive increase in the sale of mainframe computer systems for the large commercial and scientific organisations, and also growing activity in the new minicomputer market amongst the medium-sized organisations, especially those engaged in engineering and scientific applications. The mainframe market began to be dominated by a few large manufacturers who produced the hardware and system software for their products, the biggest of these manufacturers being the International Business Machines (IBM) Corporation of New York.

The other principal mainframe manufacturers were ICL in the UK, formed as a result of a merger of smaller data processing organisations; Burroughs and Univac (later Sperry Univac) in the USA; and national computer companies in France and West Germany.

The principal minicomputer manufacturer was the Data Equipment Corporation (DEC) whose first major product was the PDP-8 in the late 1960s. Later, other minicomputer manufacturers were to appear, including Data General with their NOVA and Eclipse ranges; Texas Instruments; Hewlett Packard; and others from the electronic equipment manufacturing organisations.

Around these principal manufacturing organisations grew a second level of manufacturers who effectively 'mimicked' the products of the principal manufacturers, especially those of IBM. These Plug-Compatible manufacturers offered products which were functionally identical to the main manufacturer but at a substantially reduced cost because they did not have the research and development overheads to carry. A similar 'service' was performed in the minicomputer sector by the so called Original Equipment Manufacturers (OEMs) who took advantage of the fact that minicomputers were, in general, poorly supported by the manufacturers and that, by suitable 'badge engineering' and support, the OEM could effectively supply an original product based on a DEC or Data General processor and other components. The main difference between the plug-compatibles and the OEMs was that the former were, in general, actively discouraged by the principal manufacturers concerned, whilst the latter were encouraged: it was much easier from a marketing and supply point of view for a minicomputer manufacturer to sell to an OEM rather than direct to the end-user organisation.

At the same time as the hardware advanced, software was improving but at a slower rate. The early high-level languages were consolidated and went through several versions as users demanded more and more facilities. Software development tools and utilities were developed first of all by the computer manufacturer but later by a growing body of independent software houses. The 'independents' were the software equivalents of the hardware plug-compatible manufacturers in that they exploited a growing market for providing software to the end users which competed with the 'official' computer manufacturers' offerings which were often poorly designed and supported. Again IBM was the manufacturer who attracted the most attention from the software 'plug-compatible' independent suppliers because of its high penetration of the mainframe user market.

During the 1960s the concept of the system software layer between the physical hardware and the applications program had evolved. The applications program communicated with the 'software machine' not with the physical hardware. The system software layer or operating system handled all routine processing and internal 'housekeeping' and provided a host of services to the applications programmer which further improved the development dialogue between user and machine. Other software products began to appear on the market aimed at assisting the programmer in meeting the growing demands of end users of computing services.

These end users were the accounting, engineering, personnel and other departments of organisations requiring computer-based systems to enhance or replace manual procedures. In order to efficiently service these user departments, a data processing department was usually set up to provide a centralised service. The data processing department administered the requests for computing services, hired the specialist staff required to provide computer-based solutions, and operated and maintained the computers themselves. This department had a management structure much the same as other service departments. The data processing department had to keep up with the hardware and software developments and provide an improved service, based on the latest products and techniques. At the same time the department had to ensure that existing systems were maintained and enhanced, and new systems were developed and delivered to user departments within a reasonable time frame.

Despite the continuing improvements in both the hardware and software, it became apparent that centralised data processing departments were not able to keep up with the rising demand for computer-based solutions. Many reasons have been put forward to explain why this was so and many data processing departments still regarded themselves as providing a satisfactory service but, in general, the users thought differently. Surveys carried out in the United States, and, more recently, in the United Kingdom, provide evidence of a growing problem, especially for large mainframe-based operations, in meeting user requirements.

One of the principal factors which has been identified appears to be the substantial amount of human effort required to translate a user's requirement into a computer-based system. The specialised human effort of systems analysis, design, programming and error correction and documentation – interposed between the person requiring the system and its actual implementation on the computer – leads to misunderstandings, delays and rising costs of installed systems. Furthermore those systems, after they have been installed, frequently need to be changed for one reason or another, and so there is a continuing requirement for specialist human involvement throughout the lifetime of the application. The former class of involvement is generally called development, and the latter (post-delivery) class is called maintenance.

These problems of data processing development and maintenance can be summed up by saying:

— "It costs too much";

— "It takes too long";

— "It doesn't work".

Users have reacted in two distinct ways. They either:

— do without computer-based applications and carry on with existing, often outdated and inefficient procedures;

or

— attempt to implement systems themselves, often without the involvement of the official data processing department.

In the former case, the lack of computer-based systems in areas where they would be beneficial could impair the overall effectiveness of the organisation vis-a-vis its competitors. In the latter case, there may be at best a wasteful duplication of resources, leading to a proliferation and incompatibility of systems and at worst a major system failure necessitating expensive intervention by the official data processing department.

The data processing department can, and has, responded to users' reactions by attempting to alleviate the problems associated with data processing development and maintenance. Three such approaches, not mutually exclusive, are:

— increasing existing computer resources and personnel and introducing more management control over projects;

— instituting a policy of buying in packaged software solutions where they seem to fit user requirements;

— using more automated means of producing 'tailored' application solutions and involving the end users more in the development process.

This book focuses on the third of these options, with attention to one particular approach to automated application development – that using a relatively new class of software product, the Application Program Generator (APG).

2 What is an APG?

INTRODUCTION

The term Application Program Generator (APG), as used in this book, denotes a variety of different software products with particular common features:

— they assist in application development as an alternative, or in addition, to procedural high-level languages such as COBOL, PL/1 or BASIC;

— their approach is largely non-procedural, ie concerned with 'what' is required rather than 'how' to achieve it;

— they are concerned with improving the efficiency and productivity of application development and maintenance, mainly in business data processing areas;

— they are designed to be used by a broad spectrum of developers, ranging from applications programmers through systems analysts to end users requiring the applications.

The APG approach aims to produce applications more easily, quickly and cheaply than can be achieved by other methods. The approach taken, the required computing environment, the facilities offered and the range of possible applications capable of being produced by the product vary considerably between different APGs. This is sometimes reflected in their descriptive titles such as Code Generator, Systems Generator, Applications Generator, Application Development System, etc, but sometimes this product description owes more to the marketing department of the vendor than to the product's actual technical capability.

In this chapter, APGs will be generally defined and described and the products covered by this generic term will be classified according to various criteria which reflect their approach, environment, capabilities and facilities. This classification system can then be used as a basis for comparing different products.

GENERAL OVERVIEW OF AN APG

For the purpose of this book, an Application Program Generator will be defined as follows:

— an APG is a class of software products offered as an addition or an alternative to other software products concerned with producing data processing applications. The main objective of the APG is to enable such applications to be produced more easily, cheaply and quickly then hitherto possible.

The APG attempts to meet its main objectives by providing facilities which enable the application developer to concentrate much more on 'what' an application is required to do rather than the detailed procedure of 'how' it is achieved. This 'what' rather than 'how' approach is the main distinguishing factor between an APG and a conventional high-level language such as COBOL, PL/1 or BASIC when used for application development. Such an approach is said to be 'non-procedural' since, in general, it is not concerned with procedure but with intention. Conventional high-level languages on the other hand are said to be procedural because the developer has to specify, using the particular language features, the procedure by which a particular requirement is met.

The 'higher' level of application specification mapping onto the target computer system, which is possible using an APG, reduces the amount of detailed application coding needed. Hence, developers may not require the services of an application programmer to map the application onto the target computer system and therefore one of the manual stages of application development – that of program design, code and test – is removed. This 'shortening' of the application development process leads to the benefits of easier, quicker and cheaper applications for the end user.

Figure 2.1 shows a conventional 'Victorian Novel' development process with separate distinct phases each to be completed before the next one starts, and each requiring extensive documentation to describe its output.

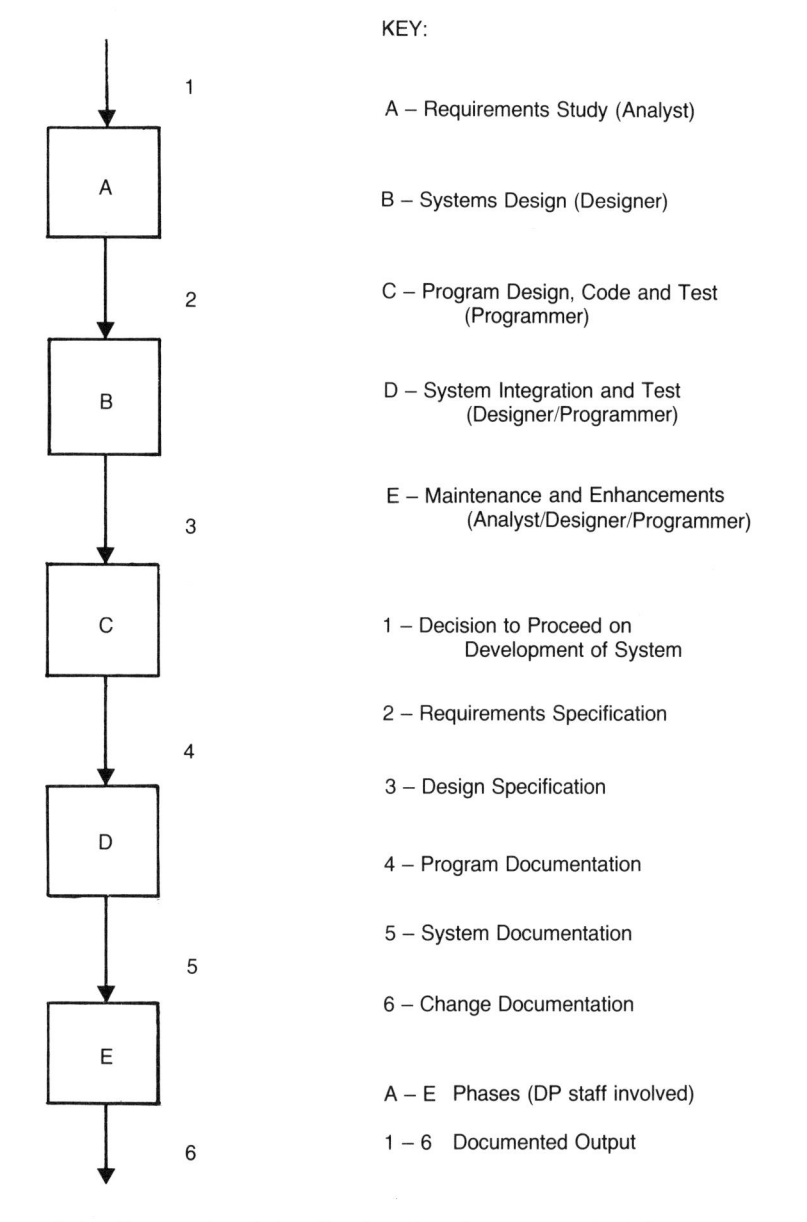

Figure 2.1 Conventional Application Development and Maintenance Life Cycle

One of the benefits claimed for APGs is that end users can participate more in the development process which, because of its shortening, can be a several-times-through interactive process rather than a once-through linear process. Such iteration reduces the need for a complete specification of requirements to be produced before detailed design commences, and hence allows users more scope to 'try before they buy' (ie test prototypes of the system before finally settling on exact requirements). This approach is more likely to produce applications which satisfy the end user, reducing the need for costly post-design changes which resulted from the user not being able to predict exact requirements at the pre-design stage.

EVOLUTION OF APGs

The concept of 'reusability' of software has been sought since the earliest times of computing. Certain 'routines', once developed, were used time and again in different applications, because they performed 'standard' tasks common to many applications. The earliest of these application-oriented routines were used to perform mathematical functions: such functions could be exactly described by standard algorithms which were refined and optimised by specialists to generate an accurate and efficiently produced result. Programmers were quite happy to use these algorithms because:

—   they did not have sufficient knowledge to program the routines from first principles;

—   they were confident that the developed algorithms could not be improved without losing the generality required in different calling programs.

Such routines were usually part of a standard program function set and were treated like program instructions, ie as macro-instructions.

A common requirement of mass business data processing was sorting and merging of data for subsequent batch transaction processing. It soon became clear that sort/merge routines could be developed which were usable by different applications. Another major data processing task thought to be a candidate for separate treatment was the formatting of reports which, because of their two dimensional nature, are awkward to program in a uni-dimensional linear language such as COBOL. Reporting was also seen as a major unvarying requirement of commercial data processing applications thus justifying the use of a separate development tool.

The arrival of teleprocessing (TP) software and the increased availability of on-line terminals brought a requirement for TP and screen programming. Special screen definition languages were developed which allowed the screen to be defined to the application. It soon became clear that the screen itself should be used to define a particular screen format rather than attempting to describe the screen in a linear fashion.

The other big development of the 1970s was the increased use of databases rather than conventional files for information storage, and also the idea of separating data from its applications. This led to the advent of Database Management Systems (DBMS) software with which the developer had to communicate using facilities within the particular language, eg 'call' level interface in COBOL. An enquiry facility was often built into the DBMS.

While these developments were taking place at the large mainframe end of data processing, very small computers were beginning to make an appearance at the other end of the scale. These 'personal' computers, equipped with up to 64K of Random Access Memory (RAM), a single terminal Visual Display Unit (VDU) and keyboard, dual floppy disks with up to 1 Mbyte capacity and a printer, were being used by managers requiring personal filing systems. Their widespread use, encouraged by the availability of powerful microprocessors on a chip and single board microcomputer systems, led to a proliferation of applications-oriented software. Standard applications packages for common financial systems were developed and sold to this new class of user 'as is' but were often not suitable for that user's particular problem and so were quickly followed by generalised file management systems and generators to enable managers to develop their own systems. These were screen-based menu-driven systems utilising many of the dialogue features of the enquiry language used with mainframe DBMS.

Today's APGs represent a continuation of these trends and an attempt, at least in some of the products, to integrate many of the previously separate elements of application development software. The modern APG can be used to produce applications requiring the production of reports, simple and ad hoc enquiries, file definition and maintenance, screen-based or form-based data input and validation, and, either via a coded exit to a conventional high-level language or using a built-in very-high-level language, procedural programming for the specific processing parts of the application.

CLASSIFICATION OF APGs

When considering what particular APG product will be most suitable for an installation it is helpful to classify a product according to relevant criteria against which its usefulness can be ascertained. In this book APGs will be classified according to computing environment, the type of output produced, the scope and method of applications, and the development facilities available.

Computing Environment

Since APGs do not, in general, operate in isolation from other software and hardware, the particular computer environment required by the APG should be ascertained. Conversely when looking for an APG, a major constraint may well be an existing environment. In either case, the installation requirements in terms of the hardware, and operating and other software are a fundamental prerequisite.

Environments for APGs vary enormously, the main ones being mini- and microcomputers and mainframes. Hence a subgroup can be classified as:

— IBM mainframes;

— other manufacturers' mainframes;

— minicomputers;

— microcomputers.

The mainframe section has been divided since IBM has many more installations than any other single manufacturer. Within these main groupings, the more specific environmental requirements of the particular product can be ascertained by reference to the product detail information.

Form of Output

Another fundamental difference between various APGs is the form of, and the conditions for executing, their applications. Two definite types of APG exist based on form of output:

— code generator;

— application generator.

Code Generator

This type of APG produces applications in the form of a high-level language source program or possibly an assembler source usually for subsequent translation and/or execution independent of the parent APG. Therefore the application is a separate piece of stand-alone software which could have been produced by hand-coded techniques.

Application Generator

This type of APG usually incorporates a translator and also controls execution of the generated application. Hence the generator and the application are both required to be present at run-time.

The Code Generator type of APG produces commonly used high-level languages such as COBOL, PL/1 or BASIC. The Application Generator type of APG either has an internal compilation facility or more usually interprets parameter tables at run-time.

Scope/Method of Applications

Four categories of scope and four possible methods have been considered, as shown in Table 2.1.

Scope	Method
— Input definition — Data definition/update — Procedure definition — Report/Enquiry definition	— Screen painting — Form filling — Questionnaire — Commands

Table 2.1   Scope/Method of Applications

Scope

The scope refers to those functional components of an application which a particular APG is capable of producing. The four major components of data processing applications are shown in Table 2.1. Some APGs have the capability of producing applications which can include any or all of those components. Other APGs are restricted in their capabilities to producing applications which do not include some of the components. A description of each functional component is given below.

Input definition is concerned with the processing requirements associated with data input, which can be carried out either on-line via special operator screens or off-line as a batch operation. Irrespective of the method of entry, certain validation and other processing tasks are normally carried out to check the data for correctness and integrity before further fundamental processing is performed. The data entry component performs the appropriate validation and other processing required.

In addition, for data entry via Visual Display Units (VDUs), the actual screens to be presented to the personnel carrying out the data entry task need to be designed, generated and transmitted. This imposes extra processing requirements on the developer including such refinements as screen formatting, automatic cursor positioning, physical field attribute setting (eg highlighting particular parts of the screen), automatic filing of particular fields or parts of fields, designation of fields as mandatory input (ie data must be entered by the operator) or as read only (ie data input not allowed), and 'forced' verification of entered data.

Many on-line applications depend on the use of multiple screens and so the flow of control from one screen to the next is an important aspect of such applications. Some APG products claim the capability to both design and connect screens to each other without recourse to significant further application programming. This is a very useful feature for prototyping these applications.

Data definition is concerned with defining, allocating and accessing the data storage structures of an application. Many APGs utilise a combination of a data dictionary (DD) and file or database management system (FMS or DBMS) software to perform these tasks.

The DD/FMS or DBMS software is either an integral part of the APG (or conversely the APG is a part of a more comprehensive integrated product which also contains a DD/FMS or DBMS), or is a separate product (or products) transparently accessible by the APG during development and by the resultant applications during execution.

Once an application's data storage requirements have been defined in the data dictionary, subsequent access of data items is largely automatic and transparent to the application. The role of the data dictionary is often extended to control access to a common files structure or database, eg which data items applications are permitted to access and the mode of access (ie read only or both read and update). This feature is particularly useful when there are several levels of user access to the common data structures (eg end users allowed to read certain data structures for enquiry/reporting).

Apart from defining an access to data structures, this component is also responsible for controlling the security and integrity of those structures.

Procedure definition provides the means of defining the particular processing requirements of an application. It is less amenable to a standard approach because of the great number of processing options which are, in general, required. Nevertheless, it is possible to perceive many processing routines which are general and reusable in numerous different applications.

APGs capable of carrying out generalised procedure definition can use three possible ways (none of which are necessarily mutually exclusive) to achieve this. They can:

— use a built-in very-high-level language (VHLL). Such procedure-definition languages generally provide the application developer using the APG with a superset of commands. These can be used for carrying out routine processing tasks involving the control structures of sequence, selection and interaction as well as the normal range of Boolean and arithmetic function operators. Such VHLLs are generally more modern in concept than conventional high-level languages (HLLs) such as COBOL, PL/1 or BASIC. They can provide the mechanisms for supporting structured programming design methodologies such as top-down design, modular programming and step-wise refinement;

— use a library of reusable code blocks. In this approach, common program structures or 'skeletons' are created using standard software components and these skeletons are then 'fleshed out' using standard data processing routines. In particular the routines can be added to by the organisation concerned and can employ company standard approaches. Typically 60% to 80% of an application's programming requirements can be handled by using this technique;

— use a standard high-level language. Where an APG does not have a procedure-definition capability or where it is required to carry out processing which is beyond the capability of the built-in facility, this approach can be adopted. The APG needs to have a capability of allowing code produced externally to be combined with that produced internally.

Report/Enquiry definition is concerned with the formatting of reports (usually output via a printer) and the generally shorter responses to on-line enquiries presented on a user's visual display unit. Report definition involves the layout of the report (ie the definition of headings, footings, margins, etc) and the report details based on existing data items. In addition, common processing tasks such as sorting, merging, averaging, totalling and the provision of breakpoints are sometimes included in the reporting component. Printing control is also an important feature of APGs which have good reporting facilities.

The structuring of on-line enquiry responses is rather different and is generally handled by those products sporting an enquiry language. The language is usually associated with those products which are designed for a database environment, allowing end users to obtain a relatively rapid response to simple and ad hoc enquiries on data held in that database.

Method

Method refers to the approach taken by a particular APG to produce the functional components of an application. Methods used vary between products and depend on the component to be produced. Four general methods which are used by most APG products are shown in Table 2.1 and are outlined below.

Screen painting uses a video display screen to simulate a screen or a page which is to be developed for an application. The APG allows the developer to configure the layout of the applications display or page (for a report) by presenting a blank screen initially on which the developer 'paints' or places, using cursor commands and keys, the required information in the appropriate positions.

When the developer has completed such a session, the screen image is translated and stored to be retrieved at the appropriate time and place within the application using it.

Screen painting, which is of course an on-line technique, is used for the data entry and other screen production components of on-line applications and can also be used for report layouts where the APG's screen is effectively simulating a page of printed report.

Form filling (or fill-in-the-blanks, as it is sometimes called) is another widely used technique for accomplishing a component definition. This method also assumes the APG utilises a visual display unit and in this case the screen presented to the developer is not blank, as for screen painting, but is pre-formatted with the available options.

The developer selects the desired options by 'filling in' parts of the pre-formatted screen and by using appropriate cursor commands and keys. On completion of such a session, the responses are stored away and are usually used to parameterise the appropriate component selection program.

Form filling, like screen painting, can be used to produce an application's screens and reports. It can also be used for other definition components, eg data definition.

The *questionnaire* approach again presumes the developer is working at a VDU. The particular aspects of the application under development are presented in the form of a series of questions requiring usually an affirmative or a negative response from the developer. At the end of a session, the resultant responses are stored away as was the case with the form filling method.

The *command language* approach is the same as that used in conventional high-level language programming except that the commands used are likely to be less procedural. This method can be used for any of the components of an application and can also be used off-line as well as on-line so in that sense it is the most flexible method. It suffers though from the general disadvantages of a command language approach ie requirement to learn the syntax, and a uni-dimensional approach to what are generally multi-dimensional problems.

Development Facilities

Many of the facilities used to support application development may also be present within the APG or may be transparently interfaced to it. The

facilities themselves and the means of invoking them form what is sometimes called a development support environment.

Two principal *invoking mechanisms* for development environment
facilities are Menus and Commands.

Menus

The menu is a well known method of providing for options within application programs and is a convenient and relatively user-friendly method of
invoking the facilities of an APG. As its name suggests, it invites the user
to select options from a list by depressing selected keys. Sometimes these
are specially provided program function keys; otherwise they are normal
alphanumeric keys.

The user selects the required option by depressing the appropriate
key(s) and is then either presented with a further menu restricted to
options within the scope of the previous one or is able to proceed with
whatever was requested. At least one of the options allows an exit from
the system.

Commands

A set of commands is the other usual method of invoking the development environment services. It has the advantage of being more convenient for an experienced developer but is less 'friendly' for the novice.

General *development support facilities* offered vary from product to
product. Some of the following are amongst those more usually offered.

Help Screens

These are screens within the development environment of on-line APGs
which can be called up to explain the effect of a particular command or
action. They in effect take the place of a manual with the advantage of
being called up from the terminal whenever required.

Split/Rotating Screens

The ability to rotate or split a screen with a command to allow more than
one logical screen to be made available on one physical VDU is a useful
facility offered in some products.

It enables a developer to look at two or more aspects of an application almost simultaneously (eg the data definitions whilst designing a data entry screen format).

Editors

An editor is an essential development aid and can either be provided by the particular APG or interfaced to it. The editor allows the particular application component to be described to the APG before it is implemented. Some APGs offer more than one editor, each being specific to the application component under development; eg a screen editor for designing screens and a special editor for use with the very-high-level language of the APG. Sometimes these editors are 'smart', ie they respond to the component under development and will not allow editing commands which are inappropriate. Syntax checking is often incorporated.

Other Utilities

Other useful utilities, such as display, print, rename, copy, etc, are also likely to be present in the development environment of APGs. The environment also provides for the transparent interfaces to external software used by the APG, eg the operating system, database management system, teleprocessing monitor, other high-level languages, etc.

CONCLUSIONS

The question posed by this chapter's title has been answered by providing a definition and general description of APGs. In addition, the evolution of this type of product has been traced since the beginning of computing up to the present time. The differences between various types of APG were examined and a classification scheme based on criteria concerned with environment, type, scope, methods and support was described.

3 Performance of APGs

INTRODUCTION

This chapter examines the evidence provided by current users of APGs in response to a questionnaire circulated during February 1983. The users were identified by APG vendors as a result of a vendor questionnaire circulated in December 1982. The user questionnaire was distributed to 99 organisations out of which 33 responses were obtained.

The returns were analysed and the findings are presented in the following sections followed by a conclusion derived from their results.

THE USER ORGANISATIONS

A reasonably broad spectrum of user organisations is represented, classified by industry sector, size, and installation details.

Industry Sector

Table 3.1 lists the number and percentage of each major industry sector grouping represented.

Size

The organisations ranged from very small companies (with under ten employees and under £100,000 annual turnover) to the very large companies (with over 5000 employees and annual turnovers in the billions of pounds range).

Installation Details

Computer Systems

The four main computer installation categories used in this book were

Sector	Number	Percentage
Manufacturing	9	27
Financial	7	21
Retail/Distribution	5	15
Government	4	12
Public Utilities	2	6
Software Houses	6	18
Total	33	99

Table 3.1

Installation	Number	Percentage
IBM Mainframe	10	30
Other Manufacturers Mainframe	7	21
Minicomputers	12	36
Microcomputers	4	12
Total	33	99

Table 3.2

represented as shown in Table 3.2.

The IBM installations included all main ranges and operating systems. The other mainframe manufacturers included Sperry Univac, Burroughs and ICL. The minicomputers included machines from DEC, Prime, Hewlett Packard, Data General and CMC. The micros were all of the single-user CP/M or equivalent type.

The installation sizes, in terms of number of terminals and main memory, ranged from the single user micro with 64K RAM through to the large mainframe with 400+ terminals and 16 Mbyte of main memory.

Development Staff

These are defined as the personnel responsible for developing the computer applications within the organisations concerned. They range in type from end users with sufficient skills to develop their own applications to data processing professionals (ie systems analysts, programmers or programmer/analysts), working within a defined data processing department within the organisation. In number they range from 1 to 150 per organisation, the average being 25.

ACQUISITION OF APGs

The process of acquiring an APG usually starts with an initial requirement formulated internally, followed by some sort of evaluation of available products culminating in the choice of the selected product. In this section, these three stages are analysed to ascertain how the respondents made their choice.

Initial Requirement

Five options were offered and the results were as shown in Table 3.3.

Reason	Number Citing
Improve application development productivity	31
Provide users with tool for own development	23
Improve user requirement satisfaction	19
Other reasons	3

Table 3.3

The 'other reasons' given were: 'to develop special application', 'to allow a distribution of software tools' and 'to demonstrate for sale to customers'.

Method of Choice

The options here and the response to each were as shown in Table 3.4.

Method	Number Citing
A formal evaluation	20
A vendor approach	9
Attendance at a seminar	7
Promotional literature perusal	7
Other	8

Table 3.4

The formal evaluation procedures are dealt with in Chapter 5 – **Evaluation of APGs**. The 'other' method mainly comprised an informal evaluation process and testing the suitability of the product in-house. One very frank reply here was that the decision to acquire the product was actually a 'political decision' taken in direct contravention to the results of a formal evaluation.

Reasons for Choice of Selected APG

The options for reason of choice of the selected APG and the responses are shown in Table 3.5.

The functional requirements were those cited under Initial Requirements, above. The 'other' options cited were price and the fact that the product was already in use in a similar capacity elsewhere in the organisation. One responder said that the reason for choice was an uninformed decision.

Reason	Number Citing
Best met the functional requirement	24
Was most compatible with existing environment	17
Was best supported by vendor	11
Was most user friendly	13
Other	6

Table 3.5

Conclusions

The procedures and method of choosing the selected APG follow the usual pattern of formulating requirements. The various competing products are evaluated, and the product is selected which is most likely to meet those requirements and also offer other benefits.

The overwhelming initial reason for wanting to acquire an APG is to improve application development productivity (31 out of 33 respondents). Surprisingly perhaps, reducing maintenance is only fourth choice, with 15. The requirement to provide users with a tool for own development was second with 23 and to improve user requirement satisfaction was third (19).

The method of choosing the selected APG was largely based on formal evaluation techniques or informal methods involving user trials. A surprisingly large number of respondents however were content to select after only a limited knowledge of the product.

The final choice was based largely on the functional requirements first cited. However, other benefits and reasons, especially the requirement for the product to be compatible with the existing environment and that it should be easy to use, were also strongly represented. Again, perhaps surprisingly, support did not rank higher than fourth choice.

APPLICATION DEVELOPMENT, EXECUTION AND MAINTENANCE

The aspects examined in this section are presented in the form of tables listing the proportions of each aspect as a percentage of the whole, both before the selected APG was acquired and after, so that a comparison can be made.

Development Methods

These are the methods using the software tools on which the development of commercial applications was based. Three major methods are given, the 'other methods' being such things as use of applications packages or development carried out by an external organisation, eg a software house. The high-level languages used were mainly COBOL, PL/1 and BASIC in that order. The results are given in Table 3.6.

Development using:	Before %	After %
High-level languages	81	40
APGs	0	58
Other methods	19	2
Total	100	100

Table 3.6

The results show the content of usage of APGs since they have been introduced into an organisation.

Application Execution Modes

This refers to the type of applications executed in terms of whether they are, first of all, batch or on-line and based on the use of conventional files or databases. Secondly it refers to whether the applications are for regular production execution or occasional ad hoc execution. The results are shown in Table 3.7.

Modes (i)	Before %	After %
Batch file	26	12
Batch database	17	17
On-line file	26	26
On-line database	31	45
Total	100	100
Modes (ii)	Before %	After %
Production	76	70
Ad hoc	24	30
Total	100	100

Table 3.7

The results show that there has been a movement away from the batch file mode of operation towards the on-line database mode with the others remaining unchanged. There is also a smaller though important change between the proportions of applications for production (reduced) as against ad hoc (increased).

Development vs Maintenance

The aspects examined here are the relative proportions of person-time spent on the development of new applications and on the maintenance of existing applications. The results are shown in Table 3.8.

The results show there is clearly a big change caused by the introduction of the APG. They tend to bear out the claims of the APG vendors that use of their products can reduce the time and resources spent on maintaining existing applications, thus allowing more to be spent on the development of new applications.

Factor	Before %	After %
Development	59	74
Maintenance	41	26
Total	100	100

Table 3.8

EFFECTS OF APG USAGE

The survey respondents were asked whether the use of their chosen APG had affected their application backlog, development productivity and use of resources. In each case they were asked to quantify or particularise the effect. Finally they were asked for a general comment on their experience of using APGs.

Application Backlog

By this is meant the time, estimated in person-years, for all the applications waiting to be developed to be produced. It includes all those applications which have already been identified, as well as an estimate of potential applications which would emerge if those currently waiting could be dealt with within a reasonable time span.

Two-thirds of the survey respondents said that the use of APGs had affected this backlog in a positive way, ie had reduced it significantly ranging from a halving to a 15 to 1 reduction in backlog compared with before the acquisition of the chosen APG.

The one-third who said that their backlog had not been reduced said things like "It's too early to tell" and "More applications keep coming in". Only one respondent cited performance problems with the chosen APG as the reason why the backlog had not been reduced.

The average size of the backlog appears to be around 166 person-years (according to provisional returns of a survey carried out by Xephon on selected UK IBM sites in early 1983), and the estimated elapsed time to deal with it, given current tools and resources, is approximately 5 years.

Application Development Productivity

The productivity measurement is defined, for the purpose of this book, as the person-time required to develop a given application. This is expressed as a ratio of conventional high-level language-based techniques to APG-based techniques.

29 out of 33 respondents reported an increase in productivity; one reported no increase; and three did not know. 28 of the 29 quantified the increase with figures between 1.2 to 1 and 15 to 1 with an average productivity improvement of 5.5 to 1.

Some examples of applications developed and relative timescales are as follows:

— a corporate budgeting system which took three months to produce using COBOL was rewritten using an APG in three weeks. Another major system which took eight person-years to produce using COBOL was rewritten in three person-years using an APG. It is three times bigger than the original system and the documentation, instead of occupying 6 ft of shelf space, is now contained in a three inch thick binder;

— a plant register system which took one person-year to develop originally was completed, by a relative novice, in two person-months;

— an estimating database was backlogged for two years and was estimated to require 2000 person-hours using conventional techniques. It was completed by two novice programmers using an APG in 2 months (ie 4 person-months).

Conclusions

The results of the user survey, if representative, provide strong evidence that APG performance is generally superior to conventional high-level language performance in application development and maintenance. APGs also have spin-off benefits of a more general nature, such as improving user/data processing relations. The main argument against these conclusions is that the results are not representative because the users were in effect 'selected' by the APG vendors.

It is certainly true that the vendors were asked to nominate up to three users for the user survey but it is not thought that there was a deliberate attempt by vendors to conceal users who were in any way dissatisfied with their chosen product. A number of users were not particularly enthralled by a product's performance and they did not hesitate to say so when this was the case. On the other hand one user thought that the questionnaire did not allow him sufficient scope to 'blow the trumpet' about the successful use of his product.

The questions asked in the survey required a direct answer and, where applicable, respondents were asked to provide examples to illustrate their response. So, apart from deliberately inventing figures and examples which does not seem likely, they would have to present factual information.

All in all, although the user survey does not pretend to be a thorough scientific investigation, it is thought to be a reasonable indication of current user experience.

4 The Vendor Survey

INTRODUCTION

The primary source of data about APG products was the questionnaire completed by vendors. The questionnaire was distributed to over 160 prospective vendors of APG products from which 58 responses were received. The data obtained was supplemented with data from other sources and resulted in the information presented in this chapter and the appendices.

In this chapter the survey method is described. The result of the response to the questionnaire is then analysed and the information presentation is described.

THE SURVEY METHOD

Identification of Vendors

One of the initial tasks of the project was to identify potential vendors of APG products. There were four main sources of information:

— computing press articles;

— software directories;

— NCC and CSA membership;

— press release.

Computing Press Articles

The NCC information abstracting service yielded a number of articles on Application Program Generators and related topics. The articles themselves listed details of a number of products and their vendors.

Software Directories

Relevant sections of general software directories such as ICP, NCC and Datapro provided further basic details of products and their vendors.

NCC and CSA Membership

A request for information about APGs was circulated to all the computer manufacturer and software vendor membership of NCC and also through the technical enquiry service of the Computing Services Association (CSA). As a result more product and vendor details were forthcoming.

Press Release

A press release was issued through the NCC press office describing the project and requesting vendors of APGs and other interested personnel to contact NCC about their possible involvement. The press release item appeared in a number of computing publications and produced more details of vendors and products.

From the four sources of information described, a mailing list of vendors was built up. The prospective vendors were then circulated, requesting basic information about all their current and soon-to-be released APG products. As a result of this exercise, a file of basic product information was built up.

The Vendor Questionnaire

Attendance at a number of seminars and discussions with actual and prospective APG users led to the design of a questionnaire for circulating to the vendors. The questionnaire design was influenced by the following objectives:

— to obtain details of the vendors and the marketing information about their APG products;

— to obtain more detailed technical information about each APG product to aid prospective acquirers in assessing suitability for their purposes.

The questionnaire approached these objectives by having two sections:

Section 1 – Summary Information
Section 2 – Detailed Product Information

Section 1 asked for general information about the vendor and the product. Section 2 concentrated on the environment, capabilities and facilities of the product and available support.

QUESTIONNAIRE RESPONSE

165 questionnaires were distributed to vendors identified on the mailing list. Of these, 58 were eventually completed and returned. In addition, one or two vendors acknowledged receipt of the questionnaire but were unable to supply the requested information.

Just over half the vendors were based overseas, mostly in the USA. A number of questionnaires were returned from the USA because the vendor was not at the address given and had not left a forwarding address. (This probably meant the vendor had ceased trading, or the original address details were incorrect.) The remainder for one reason or another just did not reply, even after a reminder was sent. They were therefore regrettably excluded from the survey.

THE SURVEY RESULTS

The completed questionnaire and other information supplied provided the basis for the product summaries, comparison and cross-reference tables and vendor details presented in the appendices. This information together with other information obtained as a result of the questionnaire responses is reviewed below.

Review of Results

The response rate of approximately 35% is reasonable considering the nature of the survey with over half the vendors based overseas. It was possible, as a result of completed questionnaires being received from overseas vendors, to identify UK agencies for some of the APG products.

Where this has been the case, the UK source has been preferred to the original. The NCC questionnaire information was supplemented by information from other sources to provide product details.

VENDORS

Most of the APG vendors are independent software suppliers, varying in size and stability from the industry 'veterans' (with a large company base and an established product line) to small new companies (with the APG as their first major software product). The remaining vendors are the software divisions of computer systems manufacturers.

PRODUCTS

The details of the products have been classified according to a number of different criteria. Where applicable, the criteria are used as a basis for comparison of the products. The major classification criteria are:

— computing environment;

— type of output;

— mode of operation;

— scope/method of application;

— support facilities.

Computing Environment

The independent software suppliers provide products which run in a variety of computer hardware and software environments although many specialise in a particular manufacturer's system. The manufacturers themselves naturally only provide products for their own systems. The environment classes for the survey are broadly defined as:

— IBM mainframe;

— other manufacturers mainframe;

— minicomputer;

— microcomputer.

IBM Mainframe

This is the largest environment category represented in the survey, as might be expected. It includes some products for which the details were obtained from another survey carried out over roughly the same period.

The majority of products for the IBM environment are supplied by independent software vendors including some of the bigger, older established companies. Many of the products add to an existing product line which includes teleprocessing systems, database management systems (DBMS), data dictionaries (DDs), etc, which effectively host the APG.

IBM themselves have three products included in the survey. The details of two of the older established products were provided by experienced users whilst IBM themselves provided details of their relational database product SQL/DS.

Most of the products will operate across the range of IBM machines and operating systems and with a variety of teleprocessing monitor, files and/or DBMS software. Some however require particular environments within both the IBM range and own supplied DBMS, DD, etc.

Other Manufacturers Mainframe

This category includes products for use in the other major mainframe manufacturers' environments, including those of ICL, Sperry Univac and Burroughs. Again there are offerings both from some of the manufacturers and also independents although the manufacturers predominate in this category. Some products which claim to be portable are also included.

Minicomputer

This category is dominated by products for Digital Equipment Corporation although DEC themselves as far as is known do not produce an APG product themselves. Other well known minicomputer environments represented are Data General, Hewlett Packard and CMC. The latter manufacturer have an APG called ALL (Application Language Liberator) which is bundled into the cost of their Sequoia System range.

Microcomputer

The response of vendors with products for the microcomputer environment was disappointing. This perhaps reflects the nature of this environment which is fast changing and very much oriented to high-turnover, low-cost products sold over the counter rather than through a manufacturer or major software house. Many of the micro-products vendors are small organisations with an unproven track record or are retail outlets without the knowledge required to supply product details for a survey.

Those vendors who have supplied details however show an interesting variety of approaches to the application development problem. One vendor, the Bristol Software Company, has a product called Silicon Office which is an attempt to integrate many of the functions of the so-called electronic office.

The micro APGs tend to be generally limited to single user operation requiring a minimal configuration of Visual Display Unit, dual floppy disk backing store and 64K words random access main memory. The range of microcomputers capable of hosting the CP/M operating system provides the largest sub-group within this environment.

Type of Output

Two basic approaches for application generation are utilised:

— generators which produce an output in the form of a high-level language source program (or sometimes assembler) which for the purpose of the survey are called code generators;

— generators which produce a directly executable application with an inbuilt translator and control subsequent execution. For the purpose of the survey these will be called application generators.

Code Generators

The source language produced by this type of APG is usually COBOL but there are some which produce other languages, principally PL/1, BAL (IBM Assembler) and BASIC. The source code produced has then to be translated (either compiled in the case of COBOL, PL/1 and BAL, or interpreted in the case of BASIC) before execution.

The principal advantage of this approach is the degree of portability achieved by separating generation from execution. The principal disadvantage is the less complete development flexibility and the degree of dependence on conventional programming skills required.

Application Generators

This kind of APG, sometimes referred to as a fourth-generation language system, usually offers a complete development and execution environment. There is no intermediate code production stage (at least not visible to the developer) and therefore debugging and other changes are generally easier to implement. This type of APG is generally an interpretive system although some compilable products also exist.

The principal advantage is the more complete development environment leading to a more user-oriented product. The principal disadvantage is the comparative lack of portability and generally increased space/time overhead of this product (although there are exceptions to this general rule).

Code generators lend themselves more readily to a traditional centralised data processing development environment and for production applications which may require tuning. Application generators are more readily accepted as a tool for end users and for ad hoc development where machine efficiency is not of a paramount concern. They are also generally better suited to prototyping or modelling applications prior to their full implementation.

Mode of Operation

Most APGs operate in an on-line environment but some are capable of batch mode operation as well. A few older products are batch only. Similarly, the applications produced by the APGs may run in one or both modes. Both APG products and their applications have therefore been classified according to their mode of operation. The potential for multi-user use of the product (re-entrant) and of its applications is also examined.

Scope/Method of Application Development

This category classifies products according to the functional parts of components. Four general data processing functional components are considered:

— input screen definition;

— file/database definition and update;

— processing definition;

— report definition.

Four principal methods of building applications for these components are considered:

— screen painting;

— form filling (fill-in-the-blanks);

— questionnaire (question and answer);

— commands (internal to the product).

Support Facilities

The support facilities include the means of communicating with the product, sometimes termed the user interface, and the development support services available as an integral part of the product.

Two principal means of invoking the product's facilities are:

— menu selection;

— commands.

These may be combined with other dialogue methods, such as some of those used for application function definition. Some products allow more than one invoking method to aid the flexibility of product use; eg menus for novice developers or end users, and commands for more experienced developers.

Two other general support facilities sometimes offered are *help screens* and *split screens*. The help screens generally provide more information about the commands or menu options allowable. Split screens improve the ease of development by allowing more than one logical screen to be viewed on one physical screen.

Other facilities which may be offered as an integral part of the product are editors, debuggers, general utilities such as print, copy, rename, etc, and transparent interfaces to a host database/data communications software environment. These and other facilities are a measure of the 'completeness' of the product.

PRODUCT SUMMARIES

A summary of each product is given in Appendix A. It includes brief classification details as outlined in the preceding sections, and it also includes additional information on terms/prices, number of installations, and a brief vendor-supplied description. Tables are provided in Appendix B for comparing facilities and capabilities.

5 Evaluation of APGs

FEASIBILITY STUDY

The decision to acquire a particular APG product is the culmination of a process which probably started with some initial reasons for considering such an acquisition. The initial reasons may have been:

— problems with current methods of application development and maintenance (see Chapter 1);

— a large expansion in the work load;

— a major upgrade or conversion to be carried out;

— a higher management directive to look at methods for cutting costs;

— the persistent attention of APG sales personnel.

Whatever the reasons are, it is always advisable to produce a coherent statement of the objectives to be achieved by any future course of action they initiate. These objectives will then form the basis of the terms of reference for a feasibility study. The main output of the feasibility study will be a document which:

— states the agreed terms of reference of the study including the objectives to be achieved;

— details the investigations which were carried out and their findings;

— lists the options possible with a brief cost/benefit analysis of each;

— concludes with a recommendation to pursue a course of action based on the option(s) providing the most beneficial possibilities.

47

The scale of the feasibility exercise naturally depends on the type of organisation and the strategic importance of the decisions to be made as a result of its conclusion. It may be no more than a discussion between colleagues resulting in a one or two page document or it could take place over a considerable length of time, involve outside consultants and result in a large detailed report for presentation at a board meeting. Whatever form it takes, the study should have at least identified the problems and examined the alternative methods of arriving at their solution. In the case of application development and maintenance problems some of the alternatives to APGs suggested in Chapter 4 were:

— to increase staffing and tighten up on existing procedures (more people and paper);

— to buy in packaged software;

— to allow end users to develop their own applications.

Each of these alternatives should be examined in sufficient detail to produce a recommendation of which one (or more than one) is 'best' for the particular organisation concerned.

STATEMENT OF REQUIREMENTS

Assuming that the feasibility study has produced a recommendation that APGs represent the 'best' approach, the next step is to look in detail at the selection criteria. The outline requirements of the feasibility study need to be expanded to a statement of conditions to be satisfied by the chosen APG product. The scale of this exercise will again depend on the particular organisation.

When considering the requirements to be fulfilled by any system, two basic questions should first be asked:

— what is meant by the requirements?

— how should the requirements be stated?

A classical answer to the first question is *requirements form the external view of the system: every detail which is visible from the outside of any system can therefore be considered a requirement.*

A requirement says nothing about *how* it is to be achieved but simply *what* must be achieved. Until such requirements have been fully defined and agreed by all interested parties within the acquiring organisation, no approach to suppliers should be made. The acquirer decides *what* is needed and the suppliers compete with *how* to achieve it.

The second question is concerned with the representation of what is required in an unambiguous form which can be readily understood by the interested parties from both the prospective acquirers and suppliers. This requires a determination to avoid jargon and provision of explanations of any unusual words or special phrases used.

The statement of requirements has two functions:

— to clarify to the acquiring organisation what conditions a product should fulfil;

— to provide the basis for an invitation to tender for prospective suppliers.

GOING OUT TO TENDER

Most organisations require more than one proposal to be obtained from prospective suppliers of any goods or services. Even where this is not an absolute requirement, it is always advisable for something which has a substantial cost element. In order that potential suppliers can quote on an equal basis there should be a straightforward document which sets out all the commercial and technical requirements to be met by potential suppliers. The statement of requirements discussed above covers the technical requirements whilst commercial details are equally important and include such things as:

— detailed costings broken down into identifiable elements;

— terms of payment;

— terms of contract and supply;

— timescales for delivery and installation;

— support details;

— user reference sites.

When completed and agreed upon, the tender document is circulated to several prospective suppliers (usually no more than six for practical purposes). Vendors of suitable products should have been identified by using the statement of requirements as an initial guide to draw up a short list. Preliminary details of products can have been obtained in a number of ways, for example as a result of contacting known suppliers, attendance at exhibitions or seminars, consulting software directories or survey reports of products such as those contained in this book.

EVALUATION OF SUPPLIERS' PROPOSALS

As a result of issuing an invitation to tender, a prospective APG acquirer should receive a number of proposals based on the acquisition of various APG products. The next task is to assess these proposals and select the product which best meets the requirements. One technique for assisting in this process is called the Weighted Ranking by Levels technique which can be used in any decision making context. A brief description of this method is given below.

Weighted Ranking by Levels

A list of factors to be considered when choosing the APG is prepared, consisting of major groups which are each split into components to produce a hierarchy of factors. The number of levels in the hierarchy depends on the level of detail required, usually up to three levels should suffice.

Each group and factor within a group should be assigned a 'weight' or proportion of importance decided on by the prospective acquirer. The weights should add up to 1.0 at each level. The actual weight for a factor at the lowest level considered is a multiple of the weights of all the appropriate groups at the higher levels.

Each product considered should be assigned a score of between 0 and 10 against each of the factors at the lowest level of the hierarchy. This 'raw' score should reflect how well or badly the product meets the requirement inherent in that factor; so that a score of 0 indicates the requirements of the factor are not present, a score of 10 indicates that the requirements are fully satisfied whilst the scores in between represent the comparative degree to which the requirement is met. (Note that a coarser scoring system of say 0-5 may be considered adequate for this exercise.)

The raw score obtained by each product for each factor is multiplied by the actual weight for that factor to give the 'weighted' score. At each level, the weighted scores of the relevant factors are added to give the score for the next level up. The addition of the weighted scores at the highest level gives the final score of each product.

Levels	Factors	Weights at Levels			Actual Weight	Product A		Product B		Product C	
							Suppliers' Scores				
		1	2	3		Raw	Weighted	Raw	Weighted	Raw	Weighted
2	Document		.4		.12	7	.84	5	.60	3	.36
2	Maintenance		.3		.09	6	.54	8	.72	9	.81
2	Training		.2		.06	5	.30	4	.24	2	.12
2	Installation		.1		.03	3	.09	5	.15	8	.24
1	SUPPORT	.3	1.0		.3		1.77		1.71		1.53
1	ENVIRONMENT	.2					.8		1.2		1.0
1	CAPABILITIES	.5					2.22		1.54		2.69
1	TOTALS	1.0					4.79		4.45		5.22

Note: The production of this chart as an output report would be a good test of the report producing capability of an APG.

Figure 5.1   Example of Use of Weighted Ranking by Levels Technique

A simple example of the technique is illustrated in Figure 5.1. The chart compares three suppliers and their products A, B and C. The assumed primary, level 1, factors are SUPPORT (weight 0.3), EN-VIRONMENT (weight 0.2) and CAPABILITIES (weight 0.5). The SUPPORT sub-factors at level 2 are shown and their weighted scores (produced by multiplying raw scores by actual weights) are added together to give the weighted sub-totals for SUPPORT. The ENVI-RONMENT and CAPABILITIES sub-totals are assumed to have been calculated in a similar manner and the three weighted sub-totals are then added together to give the total weighted scores shown. It can be seen that the supplier of product C has obtained the highest overall score.

The scores obtained by the various products are compared and the product with the highest score is, in theory, the most suitable one from a technical point of view. This score can be related to the 'cost' of the product by a calculation such as:

$$\text{Score/£}1000 = \frac{\text{Score} \times 1000}{\text{Total Product Cost}}$$
(calculated over a 5-year period)

This may produce a different winner based on relative costs.

The technique is used as a guideline only and should not be the only test applicable to the products. It can however be used to weed out those products not worthy of further consideration at a relatively early stage, and it provides an objective way of ensuring that all relevant factors are considered with a proper appreciation of their relative importance.

Testing the Products

Products which score relatively well using the Weighted Ranking by Levels technique should be considered further: other products may be ruled out at this stage.

A good way of testing both the products' capabilities and the vendors' resources is to devise a test which reflects the type of work required of the product by the acquiring organisation. If possible, some figures for producing a required application by existing methods should be available to use as a comparison with the results achieved by each product in the test. Vendors should be informed that they will be required to carry out such a test and of the conditions under which it is to be conducted.

A full day will probably be required for each test which should commence with a brief presentation of the requirements. The vendor should then be provided with the specification and allowed to attempt to produce the required application using his APG product in a given timescale.

The same test under identical conditions should be given to each of the vendors whose products are still being considered. The results should be carefully assessed and hopefully a clear winner will emerge. If there is still more than one product remaining after this first round of tests, a stiffer test lasting perhaps one week may be devised for the remaining contenders or the decision may be made on other grounds.

TRIAL OF PRODUCT

Once a product has emerged as being superior, the acquisition arrangements should be finalised. It is still possible even at this stage that there are implications far reaching enough to cause a delay to acquisition.

Many suppliers offer a free trial facility for their product, and those that do not are usually willing to arrange a rental agreement over a limited period of time so that the capabilities of the product can be fully assessed and staff can familiarise themselves with the product. If at the end of the trial or rental period the acquirer is satisfied with the product, a longer term agreement of rental or purchase can be negotiated.

6 The Future and Conclusions

INTRODUCTION

In this final chapter, possible future trends in application development software products are examined. This is followed by a summary of the findings and some conclusions which can be drawn from the project as a whole.

The examination of future trends will present two main views; an essentially short term view based on existing hardware technology and software product lines, and a longer term view based on current research into new hardware technologies and software concepts. The short term view looks at changes likely to be realised within the next two or three years whilst the longer term view looks at the period from about 1985 until the end of the current decade. No attempt is made at a longer term forecast than this, since it is unlikely to be of value and such long term forecasts have a habit of being invalidated by totally unforeseen events which produce what Americans are apt to call 'a whole new ball game'.

SHORT TERM VIEW

This short term forecast will concentrate on existing APG products in the mainframe, mini- and microcomputer environments.

Mainframe Environment

The discernable trend in this environment is towards a more integrated and easier to use set of development facilities complete with tight central-ised control of access based on an active global data dictionary/directory.

The data dictionary/directory is a basic requirement for this type of product. It is needed to document, control, monitor and upgrade data and programs as well as provide the control and audit of all applications development. The dictionary binds all the activities together by providing in one place all the meta-data concerning existing and new applications. An added use of the dictionary/directory is the authorisation control for accessing and changing data, programs and authorisation levels themselves.

Other components of the advanced APG for the mainframe environment are discussed below.

A Very-High-Level Language

The language which is the means of communicating the developer's intention should contain all the statements for data handling and arithmetic found in existing business-oriented high-level languages such as COBOL, plus effective sub-languages for database management, communications control and report generation. Such a language should generally provide non-procedural declarations of common logical tasks. Logical database definitions will be extracted directly from the data dictionary/directory component whilst screen definitions and report layouts should be fully integrated with the communications and reporting sub-languages respectively.

The procedural definition part of the very-high-level language will be based on modern program design and development methodologies. It will support features such as top-down design and modular programming, and use only the basic control constructs of sequence, selection and iteration.

An Integrated Support Environment

The very-high-level language should be contained within a development and execution support environment providing libraries, editors, utilities and on-line facilities such as translation, execution and debugging.

The environment should be capable of being invoked in a number of ways allowing for the different levels of expertise of its users. The editors should be both general purpose and specialised depending on the current development activity. Various levels of help facilities should be provided to assist developers, and it should be possible to quickly access the different parts of an application's screens, data definitions, etc by simple devices such as a screen splitting or alternative screens command.

The environment should be fully integrated with the dictionary/ directory so that user authorisation can be checked and, if so authorised, the various parts of an application can be accessed, and the control and status information in the resource model can be automatically updated. The translation, execution and debugging facilities should provide for the rapid checking of the modules of the application and for progressive integration of those modules until the whole application is completed. It should be possible for more than one developer to be simultaneously employed on the same application so that parallel development can proceed on the application or on different applications which use common modules.

The applications so developed should be capable of being run independently of the host development environment for the production versions. It should be possible to integrate conventionally developed applications with those developed via the APG, and the APG applications should be portable and independent of underlying database management systems, teleprocessing monitors and operating systems software.

Some of the more modern of the current APGs within the mainframe environment section of the survey meet some of the criteria for future products outlined above but, as far as is known, no single product currently available meets all of the criteria.

Minicomputer Environment

Future APGs for this environment will exhibit many of the characteristics of the mainframe products. Indeed such products should, together with the applications they produce, be capable of migrating from a mini to a mainframe environment to allow for hardware upgrading. To do this they will, in all probability, be hosted by portable operating systems such as PICK or UNIX.

Minicomputer-based products should also be capable of operating in a distributed computing environment. Because of the limitations on storage imposed by this environment, minicomputer APGs will be economical in the use of memory space. They will probably contain re-entrant routines which will be shared between various application components and users.

Microcomputer APGs

APGs for this environment need to be particularly suited to non-computer end users. They will tend to provide basic data processing functions for file creation, updating and maintenance, data entry and reporting.

Although primarily for use on single user systems, such future micro APGs will support networking and the use of shared resources, and provide for text as well as data manipulation.

LONGER TERM VIEW

The period from about 1985 until the end of the decade will see the emergence of software tools based on the 'Expert System' approach. An expert system has been defined as *a computing system which embodies organised knowledge concerning some specific area of human expertise, sufficient to perform as a skilful and cost effective consultant.* It usually consists of three parts:

— a database of the expert's rules-of-thumb often known as the 'knowledge base';

— a generalised program which interprets the rules in the knowledge base, called an 'inference engine';

— a database of facts particular to the current problem or consultation.

Expert systems usually employ the expert's knowledge in the form of production rules, ie with the following structure:

IF (condition) THEN (action)

The inference engine may work through the rules from the top down by choosing a goal and trying to prove it. Proving the chosen goal involves finding it in the (action) part of a rule and trying to show that (condition) is true. Since this appears to be using the rules backwards, this type of control structure is known as backwards chaining, or goal-directed reasoning. It has the advantage that the questions asked of the user appear to 'home-in' on the answer as the consultation progresses. However, it may not always be possible to choose a likely goal initially, and the reverse form of control, forward chaining or data-driven reasoning, or a combination of goal- and data-directed control, may need to be used.

Many expert systems are able to reason with uncertain information. There are a number of techniques which permit this ranging from simple probability theory, through Bayesian reasoning to what is known as 'fuzzy' logic. The system will generally have to justify its line of reasoning to the user. To do this there is normally a user-friendly interface contained within the inference engine.

The expert system can not only capture and communicate expertise but can also learn from further experience. Japan has recognised that such 'humanised' computers are an essential key to the goal of the information society and have launched a ten year programme to realise that goal by developing what have become known as fifth generation computers.

The Japanese fifth generation computer programme includes elements of design and development into:

— very large scale integrated circuits (VLSI);

— distributed 'parallel' processing architectures;

— expert systems.

It is hoped that the fruits of these design and development projects can be brought together to produce radically new computer systems for the 1990s and beyond.

The United States and Europe have now recognised the dangers of allowing Japan to develop such a lead in this area and have launched their own programmes of research and development along similar lines to the Japanese programme.

The implications of expert systems, especially when coupled with advanced computer systems, to conventional data processing are enormous. They are a practical yet fundamental innovation in the storage, refinement, distribution and use of a problem-solving ability. Because expert systems present a potentially very user-friendly interface they will be a pervasive innovation with roles to play in every sector and level of the economy.

The market for building, refining and selling expert systems applications is likely to be very big business for the software services industry by 1990. Revenue will come from business, government and consumer markets and go largely to small specialist expert system builders, professionals who supply the basic expertise and common carriers. Another major market is likely to be in the gradual re-orientation of conventional software to an expert systems approach.

There are a number of expert systems based on conventional computers already in existence, and others are being developed or planned (see Table 6.1). Most of these systems are prototypes but some are already providing valuable information in their specific areas.

SUMMARY AND CONCLUSIONS

The project to survey software products called Application Program Generators established that there were in existence at least 70 such products, details of which were collected and recorded. It is estimated that there are probably the same number again whose details have not been recorded in this survey.

After examining the background and historical development of APGs as described in Chapter 1, the project next looked at the characteristics of these products which distinguished them from other software development products. This was achieved by the definition and description of an APG product which is set out in Chapter 2. The APG products themselves were then classified according to various criteria to enable a basic evaluation of their characteristics to be made and to distinguish between different sub-groups of products which met the general definition criteria.

A classification system emerged based on environment, output, scope/method and development support facilities of the products. This system has enabled the compilation of product profiles and comparison tables, both of which are contained in the Appendices.

The performance capabilities of APGs have been examined by reference both to published case studies and by commissioning a survey of users, the outcome of which is set down in Chapter 3. The survey showed that, by and large, users were benefiting from APGs although there was still room for improvement.

Chapters 4 and 5 described the survey method used and evaluated the results obtained to provide prospective acquirers with general information on the use of feasibility studies and selection techniques.

The final chapter is concerned with the future of APGs in both the short and longer term. From this it can be seen that APGs should continue to improve in performance and facilities. They will probably

(a)

Application area	Name	Origin	Comments
Mineral exploration	Prospector	SRI International	Interprets surface geology prior to test drilling
Materials handling	–	British Leyland	Microcomputer ES to help select handling techniques
Mass spectral analysis	Dendral	Stanford University	First ES (1965) interprets mass spectra (chemical analysis)
Medical test analysis	Puff	Stanford University	In routine use for diagnosing pulmonary diseases
Oil platform faults	AL/X	Edinburgh University	Diagnoses automatic shutdowns
Plant pathology	AQ11	Illinois University	Exceeds human diagnosis of soyabean diseases
Medicine	Psyco	Imperial Cancer Research (UK)	Diagnoses dyspepsia
Tax advice	Tax advisor	Illinois University	Advice on capital transfer tax
Science	Conche	Leeds University	Aids scientific theory formation
System design	R1	Carnegie Mellon University	Configures DEC VAX/780 computer systems
Fault diagnosis	Crib	ICL	Diagnoses computer hardware and software faults
Medicine	Mycin	Stanford University	Diagnosis and drug treatment – better than humans in cases of multiple diseases. Mycin 'framework' also usable for developing different ESs
Education	Guidon	Stanford University	Tutor – improves students' diagnostic skills

(b)

Application area	Name	Origin	Comments
Policy analysis	–	British Telecom	Sophisticated management graphics interface working on existing planning model
Risk analysis	–	SPL International (UK)	
Command and control	–	ASWE	Naval Command and Control
Software engineering	–	Many in US and UK	Links to robotics automatic programming

Table 6.1 (a) Some Expert Systems Applications in Existence
(b) Expert Systems Applications Being Developed or Planned

provide the main development thrust, gradually taking over from conventional high-level languages, until approximately 1990. During the second half of the decade, expert systems will begin to make an impact on data processing, possibly necessitating the revision of ways of working and organisation.

APGs may not be the answer to every data processing manager's prayer for the perfect product providing maintenance-free applications on tap. It would, however, be extremely short-sighted of any data processing-using organisation to ignore the potential contribution such products are capable of making, now and in the future, to the current problems of application development and maintenance.

Appendix A

Product Summary Details

The following pages each comprise a summary of an APG product. The summary is structured as follows:

NAME — Name or acronym of the product

VENDOR — Name of principal supplier (if more than one) for UK

H/W — The computer manufacturer or type which hosts the product

OS — Operating system required (if applicable)

TPM — Teleprocessing monitor required (if applicable)

OTHER — Other software requirements or options for hosting the product

TYPE — The type classification of the product is indicated by an asterisk placed after the appropriate options. The given options are TRANSLATOR: COMPILER and INTERPRETER, and CODE GENERATOR: COBOL, PL/1, BASIC, ASSEMBLER and OTHER (other language not included in the preceding list)

EXECUTION MODE — The mode is indicated by an asterisk placed after the appropriate options which are UNDER PRODUCT and/or INDEPENDENTLY

OPERATION MODE

This comprises a matrix with 3 columns labelled BATCH, ON-LINE and MULTI-USER, and 2 rows labelled PRODUCT and APPLICATION. The modes applying to the product and the applications it generates are indicated by an asterisk in the appropriate row, column position of the matrix

SCOPE/METHOD

This comprises a matrix with 4 columns labelled DEFINITION OF: SCREENS, DATA, PROCESSING and REPORTS, and 4 rows labelled BY: SCREEN PAINTING, FORM FILLING, QUESTIONNAIRE and COMMANDS. An asterisk in the appropriate row, column position indicates which, if any, of the options apply to the product

DEVELOPMENT ENVIRONMENT

The method used in the product for invoking the environment is indicated by an asterisk following one or more of three given options INVOKED BY: MENUS, COMMANDS and OTHER. The FACILITIES contained within the environment are similarly indicated by an asterisk following the options HELP (help screens available), S/R (split-rotating) SCREENS (logical screen commands available to allow more than one aspect of an application to be viewed simultaneously), EDITORS, DEBUGGING and OTHER UTILITIES. The capability of transparently interfacing the product to other software is indicated by an asterisk following the relevant options INTERFACE TO: DBMS (database management system software), TPM (teleprocessing monitor software) and OTHER SOFTWARE

PRICE/TERMS

The appropriate amount for acquiring the product is given, but this item is included as a guide only and the actual cost should be ascertained from the vendor at the relevant time

INSTALLATIONS

The NUMBER of installations of the product, as supplied by the vendor, is given in the categories WORLD-WIDE (that is, outside the UK) and IN UK, along with the period of time that this refers to under the headings FROM, TO. Where this information is not given it should be ascertained from the vendor. In some cases, for example for a new product, it is not appropriate

DESCRIPTION

A brief description of the product is given, as supplied by the vendor.

NAME ACT/1	**VENDOR** WESTINGHOUSE

H/W IBM	**OS** VSE VM MVS	**TPM** VARIOUS	**OTHER**

TYPE	TRANSLATOR		CODE GENERATOR				
	Compiler	Interpreter	Cobol	PL/1	Basic	Assembler	Other
	*	*	*	*			

EXECUTION MODE		**OPERATION MODE**	Batch	On-line	Multi-user
Under Product	*	Product		*	*
Independently		Application		*	

SCOPE/ METHOD		DEFINITION OF:			
		Screens	Data	Processing	Reports
BY:	Screen Painting	*			
	Form Filling				
	Questionnaire				
	Commands				

DEVELOPMENT ENVIRONMENT	OPTIONS		
INVOKED BY:	Menus *	Commands	Other
FACILITIES	Help *	S/R Screens *	Editors *	Debugging *	Other Utilities
INTERFACE TO:	DBMS	TPM *	Other Software *

PRICE/TERMS On application

INSTALLATIONS	NUMBER	FROM	TO
WORLD-WIDE	55	1/01/79	31/12/82
IN UK			

DESCRIPTION An application development tool intended to help those companies building on-line applications lower the cost of application development cycle; increase user satisfaction and confidence in DP; lower the cost of application maintenance.

NAME ADAM	VENDOR CACI

H/W IBM	OS OS DOS	TPM CICS	OTHER VSAM DL/1

TYPE	TRANSLATOR		CODE GENERATOR				
	Compiler	Interpreter	Cobol	PL/1	Basic	Assembler	Other
			*				

EXECUTION MODE		OPERATION MODE	Batch	On-line	Multi-user
Under Product		Product	*	*	*
Independently	*	Application	*	*	*

SCOPE/ METHOD		DEFINITION OF:			
		Screens	Data	Processing	Reports
BY:	Screen Painting				
	Form Filling				
	Questionnaire				
	Commands	*	*	*	*

DEVELOPMENT ENVIRONMENT	OPTIONS				
INVOKED BY:	Menus *		Commands		Other
FACILITIES	Help	S/R Screens	Editors	Debugging	Other Utilities
INTERFACE TO:	DBMS *		TPM *		Other Software *

PRICE/TERMS From $80,000 to $250,000

INSTALLATIONS	NUMBER	FROM	TO
WORLD-WIDE			
IN UK			

DESCRIPTION: Advanced Developed Aids and Methods (ADAM) system for the IBM environment. New product.

NAME ADF	VENDOR IBM

H/W IBM	OS VS1 MVS	TPM IMS/DC	OTHER IMS/DB

TYPE	TRANSLATOR		CODE GENERATOR				
	Compiler	Interpreter	Cobol	PL/1	Basic	Assembler	Other
	*	*					

EXECUTION MODE		OPERATION MODE	Batch	On-line	Multi-user
Under Product	*	Product	*	*	*
Independently		Application	*	*	*

SCOPE/ METHOD		DEFINITION OF:			
		Screens	Data	Processing	Reports
BY:	Screen Painting				
	Form Filling				
	Questionnaire				
	Commands	*	*	*	

DEVELOPMENT ENVIRONMENT	OPTIONS				
INVOKED BY:	Menus		Commands		Other
FACILITIES	Help	S/R Screens	Editors	Debugging	Other Utilities
INTERFACE TO:	DBMS *		TPM *		Other Software

PRICE/TERMS On application

INSTALLATIONS	NUMBER	FROM	TO
WORLD-WIDE			
IN UK			

DESCRIPTION: A facility which makes it possible to generate IMS/VS applications quickly. Many standard programming functions can be invoked easily by entering parameters in ADF's tables, eg for screen formatting, auditing input, retrieving and updating database records. It is also possible to invoke conventionally programmed routines.

NAME	ADMINS/V32	VENDOR	CELERITY

H/W DEC VAX	OS VMS	TPM	OTHER DECNET

TYPE	TRANSLATOR		CODE GENERATOR				
	Compiler	Interpreter	Cobol	PL/1	Basic	Assembler	Other
		*					

EXECUTION MODE		OPERATION MODE	Batch	On-line	Multi-user
Under Product	*	Product		*	*
Independently		Application		*	*

SCOPE/ METHOD		DEFINITION OF:			
		Screens	Data	Processing	Reports
BY:	Screen Painting				
	Form Filling	*	*		*
	Questionnaire				
	Commands			*	

DEVELOPMENT ENVIRONMENT	OPTIONS				
INVOKED BY:	Menus		Commands		Other *
FACILITIES	Help	S/R Screens	Editors	Debugging	Other Utilities
INTERFACE TO:	DBMS		TPM		Other Software *

PRICE/TERMS	On application

INSTALLATIONS	NUMBER	FROM	TO
WORLD-WIDE	130	1/01/75	31/12/82
IN UK	10	1/01/79	31/12/82

DESCRIPTION: A fourth generation language enabling complete business and information systems to be implemented with the programming stage of systems development completely eliminated. The product is oriented towards a combined user/systems analyst development team allowing fast system development.

NAME	ADS/0	VENDOR	CULLINANE

H/W	IBM	OS	VARIOUS	TPM	VARIOUS	OTHER	IDMS

TYPE	TRANSLATOR		CODE GENERATOR				
	Compiler	Interpreter	Cobol	PL/1	Basic	Assembler	Other
	*						

EXECUTION MODE		OPERATION MODE	Batch	On-line	Multi-user
Under Product	*	Product	*	*	*
Independently		Application	*	*	*

SCOPE/ METHOD		DEFINITION OF:			
		Screens	Data	Processing	Reports
BY:	Screen Painting	*			
	Form Filling				
	Questionnaire				
	Commands			*	

DEVELOPMENT ENVIRONMENT	OPTIONS				
INVOKED BY:	Menus *		Commands		Other
FACILITIES	Help *	S/R Screens	Editors *	Debugging *	Other Utilities *
INTERFACE TO:	DBMS *		TPM *		Other Software *

PRICE/TERMS	On application

INSTALLATIONS	NUMBER	FROM	TO
WORLD-WIDE	300	1/11/81	31/12/82
IN UK	20	1/03/82	31/12/82

DESCRIPTION: Enables DP users to rapidly develop and execute on-line applications for query and update of an IDMS database or VSAM file. An active integrated data dictionary provides design, definition and documentation capabilities. Simple and complex applications can be generated and run highly efficiently.

NAME	ALL	VENDOR	CMC

H/W CMC	OS PICK	TPM	OTHER

TYPE	TRANSLATOR		CODE GENERATOR				
	Compiler	Interpreter	Cobol	PL/1	Basic	Assembler	Other
		*					

EXECUTION MODE		OPERATION MODE	Batch	On-line	Multi-user
Under Product	*	Product		*	*
Independently		Application	*	*	*

SCOPE/ METHOD		DEFINITION OF:			
		Screens	Data	Processing	Reports
BY:	Screen Painting				
	Form Filling				
	Questionnaire	*	*		*
	Commands			*	

DEVELOPMENT ENVIRONMENT	OPTIONS		
INVOKED BY:	Menus *	Commands	Other
FACILITIES	Help *	S/R Screens	Editors *	Debugging *	Other Utilities *
INTERFACE TO:	DBMS	TPM	Other Software *

PRICE/TERMS	£15,000 or bundled with hardware

INSTALLATIONS	NUMBER	FROM	TO
WORLD-WIDE	30	1/02/82	31/12/82
IN UK	12	1/09/82	31/12/82

DESCRIPTION: Dictionary driven application generator generating applications directly (not code/program generator). Complete environment covering screens, input, enquiries, reports and menus.

NAME	APPBUILD	VENDOR	DMW

H/W	IBM DEC NIXDORF	OS	VARIOUS	TPM	VARIOUS	OTHER	VARIOUS

TYPE	TRANSLATOR		CODE GENERATOR				
	Compiler	Interpreter	Cobol	PL/1	Basic	Assembler	Other
			*	*			*

EXECUTION MODE			OPERATION MODE	Batch	On-line	Multi-user
Under Product			Product	*	*	*
Independently	*		Application	*	*	*

SCOPE/ METHOD		DEFINITION OF:			
		Screens	Data	Processing	Reports
BY:	Screen Painting				
	Form Filling	*	*		*
	Questionnaire				
	Commands			*	

DEVELOPMENT ENVIRONMENT	OPTIONS				
INVOKED BY:	Menus *		Commands		Other
FACILITIES	Help *	S/R Screens	Editors *	Debugging *	Other Utilities
INTERFACE TO:	DBMS *		TPM *		Other Software *

PRICE/TERMS	£40,000

INSTALLATIONS	NUMBER	FROM	TO
WORLD-WIDE	2		31/12/82
IN UK	1		31/12/82

DESCRIPTION: A non-procedural data dictionary driven generator of complete commercial teleprocessing and batch processing application systems. The design objective is to create systems as good as could be produced by a team of good application programmers.

NAME	AUTOCODE	VENDOR	STEMMOS

H/W	MICRO	OS	CP/M	TPM		OTHER	DBAW-2

TYPE	TRANSLATOR		CODE GENERATOR				
	Compiler	Interpreter	Cobol	PL/1	Basic	Assembler	Other
							*

EXECUTION MODE		OPERATION MODE	Batch	On-line	Multi-user
Under Product		Product		*	
Independently	*	Application		*	

SCOPE/ METHOD		DEFINITION OF:			
		Screens	Data	Processing	Reports
BY:	Screen Painting				
	Form Filling				
	Questionnaire	*	*		*
	Commands				

DEVELOPMENT ENVIRONMENT	OPTIONS				
INVOKED BY:	Menus *		Commands		Other
FACILITIES	Help	S/R Screens	Editors	Debugging	Other Utilities
INTERFACE TO:	DBMS		TPM		Other Software *

PRICE/TERMS	£120

INSTALLATIONS	NUMBER	FROM	TO
WORLD-WIDE			
IN UK	450	1/06/82	31/12/82

DESCRIPTION: File management and applications generator utilising advanced data handling techniques under DBase-2.

NAME CARS	VENDOR SAGE

H/W PORTABLE	OS VARIOUS	TPM VARIOUS	OTHER VARIOUS

TYPE	TRANSLATOR		CODE GENERATOR				
	Compiler	Interpreter	Cobol	PL/1	Basic	Assembler	Other
			*				

EXECUTION MODE		OPERATION MODE	Batch	On-line	Multi-user
Under Product		Product	*		
Independently	*	Application	*		

SCOPE/ METHOD		DEFINITION OF:			
		Screens	Data	Processing	Reports
BY:	Screen Painting				
	Form Filling				
	Questionnaire				
	Commands		*	*	*

DEVELOPMENT ENVIRONMENT	OPTIONS				
INVOKED BY:	Menus		Commands		Other
FACILITIES	Help	S/R Screens	Editors	Debugging	Other Utilities
INTERFACE TO:	DBMS		TPM		Other Software

PRICE/TERMS $20,000 (US price)

INSTALLATIONS	NUMBER	FROM	TO
WORLD-WIDE	400	1/01/72	31/12/82
IN UK	8	1/01/75	31/12/82

DESCRIPTION: Computer Audit Retrieval and report generating system.

NAME	CMS	VENDOR	CML

H/W DATA GENERAL	OS DG VARIOUS	TPM	OTHER BUS.BASIC

TYPE	TRANSLATOR		CODE GENERATOR				
	Compiler	Interpreter	Cobol	PL/1	Basic	Assembler	Other
					*		

EXECUTION MODE		OPERATION MODE	Batch	On-line	Multi-user
Under Product		Product		*	*
Independently	*	Application		*	*

SCOPE/ METHOD		DEFINITION OF:			
		Screens	Data	Processing	Reports
BY:	Screen Painting				
	Form Filling				
	Questionnaire	*	*		*
	Commands			*	

DEVELOPMENT ENVIRONMENT	OPTIONS				
INVOKED BY:	Menus *		Commands		Other
FACILITIES	Help *	S/R Screens	Editors	Debugging	Other Utilities
INTERFACE TO:	DBMS		TPM		Other Software *

PRICE/TERMS	From £950

INSTALLATIONS	NUMBER	FROM	TO
WORLD-WIDE	4	1/04/81	30/11/82
IN UK	20	1/09/80	11/12/82

DESCRIPTION: Decision support system.

NAME COBMAN	VENDOR COBRA

H/W ICL, ATLAS, IBM	OS VARIOUS	TPM VARIOUS	OTHER COBOL

TYPE	TRANSLATOR		CODE GENERATOR				
	Compiler	Interpreter	Cobol	PL/1	Basic	Assembler	Other
			*				

EXECUTION MODE		OPERATION MODE	Batch	On-line	Multi-user
Under Product		Product	*	*	
Independently	*	Application	*	*	*

SCOPE/ METHOD		DEFINITION OF:			
		Screens	Data	Processing	Reports
BY:	Screen Painting				
	Form Filling				
	Questionnaire				
	Commands	*	*		*

DEVELOPMENT ENVIRONMENT	OPTIONS		
INVOKED BY:	Menus	Commands	Other
FACILITIES	Help	S/R Screens	Editors	Debugging	Other Utilities
INTERFACE TO:	DBMS *	TPM *	Other Software *

PRICE/TERMS   From £3,000 to £15,000 for annual licence

INSTALLATIONS	NUMBER	FROM	TO
WORLD-WIDE			
IN UK	12	1/07/80	31/12/82

DESCRIPTION: High level extensions to COBOL link user-written COBOL procedures into a dynamically structured program. A typical COBMAN program needs only 20% – 60% as much code as the pure COBOL equivalent.

NAME	COBOL/DL	VENDOR	ADR

H/W	IBM	OS	VSE VS1 MVS	TPM	VARIOUS	OTHER	COBOL

TYPE	TRANSLATOR		CODE GENERATOR				
	Compiler	Interpreter	Cobol	PL/1	Basic	Assembler	Other
			*				

EXECUTION MODE		OPERATION MODE	Batch	On-line	Multi-user
Under Product		Product	*	*	
Independently	*	Application	*	*	

SCOPE/ METHOD		DEFINITION OF:			
		Screens	Data	Processing	Reports
BY:	Screen Painting				
	Form Filling				
	Questionnaire				
	Commands		*	*	*

DEVELOPMENT ENVIRONMENT	OPTIONS		
INVOKED BY:	Menus *	Commands	Other
FACILITIES	Help *	S/R Screens	Editors	Debugging	Other Utilities
INTERFACE TO:	DBMS *	TPM *	Other Software *

PRICE/TERMS	On application

INSTALLATIONS	NUMBER	FROM	TO
WORLD-WIDE	25	1/01/81	31/12/82
IN UK			

DESCRIPTION: A high level extension to the COBOL language based on ADR's successful MetaCOBOL product – the industry's most widely used COBOL generator. It insulates the COBOL programmer from the physical DB/DC interface.

NAME CODE	VENDOR SHUBROOKS

H/W IBM	OS OS DOS	TPM CICS	OTHER COBOL

TYPE	TRANSLATOR		CODE GENERATOR				
	Compiler	Interpreter	Cobol	PL/1	Basic	Assembler	Other
			*				

EXECUTION MODE		OPERATION MODE	Batch	On-line	Multi-user
Under Product		Product	*	*	
Independently	*	Application	*	*	*

SCOPE/ METHOD		DEFINITION OF:			
		Screens	Data	Processing	Reports
BY:	Screen Painting				
	Form Filling				
	Questionnaire				
	Commands	*	*	*	*

DEVELOPMENT ENVIRONMENT	OPTIONS				
INVOKED BY:	Menus		Commands		Other
FACILITIES	Help	S/R Screens	Editors	Debugging	Other Utilities
INTERFACE TO:	DBMS		TPM		Other Software

PRICE/TERMS To be announced

INSTALLATIONS	NUMBER	FROM	TO
WORLD-WIDE			
IN UK			

DESCRIPTION: Cobol program generator and MAP assembler generator.

NAME COGEN	VENDOR RX

H/W NCR	OS IRX VRX IMOS	TPM VIMOS	OTHER

TYPE	TRANSLATOR		CODE GENERATOR				
	Compiler	Interpreter	Cobol	PL/1	Basic	Assembler	Other
			*				

EXECUTION MODE			OPERATION MODE	Batch	On-line	Multi-user
Under Product			Product			
Independently	*		Application			

SCOPE/ METHOD		DEFINITION OF:			
		Screens	Data	Processing	Reports
BY:	Screen Painting				
	Form Filling				
	Questionnaire				
	Commands				

DEVELOPMENT ENVIRONMENT	OPTIONS				
INVOKED BY:	Menus		Commands		Other
FACILITIES	Help	S/R Screens	Editors	Debugging	Other Utilities
INTERFACE TO:	DBMS		TPM		Other Software

PRICE/TERMS   From £3,650

INSTALLATIONS	NUMBER	FROM	TO
WORLD-WIDE			
IN UK			

DESCRIPTION: A Cobol code generator.

NAME CPG	VENDOR ALTERGO

H/W IBM	OS VSE VS1 MVS	TPM CICS SHAD2	OTHER

TYPE	TRANSLATOR		CODE GENERATOR				
	Compiler	Interpreter	Cobol	PL/1	Basic	Assembler	Other
	*					*	

EXECUTION MODE		OPERATION MODE	Batch	On-line	Multi-user
Under Product	*	Product		*	
Independently	*	Application	*	*	

SCOPE/ METHOD		DEFINITION OF:			
		Screens	Data	Processing	Reports
BY:	Screen Painting	*			
	Form Filling		*		
	Questionnaire				
	Commands			*	*

DEVELOPMENT ENVIRONMENT	OPTIONS				
INVOKED BY:	Menus *		Commands		Other
FACILITIES	Help *	S/R Screens	Editors *	Debugging *	Other Utilities
INTERFACE TO:	DBMS *		TPM *		Other Software *

PRICE/TERMS	From $24,000 to $30,000 (US price)

INSTALLATIONS	NUMBER	FROM	TO
WORLD-WIDE	500	1/01/74	31/12/82
IN UK			

DESCRIPTION: An on-line program generator designed to enable quick and efficient development of on-line systems to run in conjunction with CICS or SHADOW II. The language is based on an RPG syntax. Included in the package is an on-line program entry facility COPE with full language syntax checking.

NAME CUPID	VENDOR TUBS

H/W DEC	OS VMS RSTS RSX	TPM	OTHER

TYPE	TRANSLATOR		CODE GENERATOR				
	Compiler	Interpreter	Cobol	PL/1	Basic	Assembler	Other
		*					

EXECUTION MODE		OPERATION MODE	Batch	On-line	Multi-user
Under Product	*	Product		*	*
Independently		Application	*	*	*

SCOPE/ METHOD		DEFINITION OF:			
		Screens	Data	Processing	Reports
BY:	Screen Painting				
	Form Filling	*	*	*	*
	Questionnaire				
	Commands				

DEVELOPMENT ENVIRONMENT	OPTIONS				
INVOKED BY:	Menus		Commands		Other
FACILITIES	Help	S/R Screens	Editors *	Debugging	Other Utilities
INTERFACE TO:	DBMS		TPM		Other Software

PRICE/TERMS   From £2,000 to £13,000

INSTALLATIONS	NUMBER	FROM	TO
WORLD-WIDE	10	1/01/80	6/12/82
IN UK	30	1/01/78	6/12/82

DESCRIPTION: Application system development aid.

NAME DATAPLAN	VENDOR CSS

H/W DATA GENERAL	OS DG VARIOUS	TPM	OTHER BUS.BASIC

TYPE	TRANSLATOR		CODE GENERATOR				
	Compiler	Interpreter	Cobol	PL/1	Basic	Assembler	Other
					*		

EXECUTION MODE		OPERATION MODE	Batch	On-line	Multi-user
Under Product		Product		*	*
Independently	*	Application		*	*

SCOPE/ METHOD		DEFINITION OF:			
		Screens	Data	Processing	Reports
BY:	Screen Painting				
	Form Filling				
	Questionnaire				
	Commands	*	*	*	*

DEVELOPMENT ENVIRONMENT	OPTIONS				
INVOKED BY:	Menus		Commands		Other
FACILITIES	Help	S/R Screens	Editors	Debugging	Other Utilities
INTERFACE TO:	DBMS		TPM		Other Software

PRICE/TERMS   From £3,950 for full system

INSTALLATIONS	NUMBER	FROM	TO
WORLD-WIDE			
IN UK	6	1/01/81	31/12/82

DESCRIPTION: A program generator which produces structured Business BASIC programs from near-English sentences and is capable of handling file creation, maintenance, entry and processing of transactions and the production of reports.

NAME DELTA	VENDOR DELTA

H/W PORTABLE	OS VARIOUS	TPM VARIOUS	OTHER COBOL or PL/1

TYPE	TRANSLATOR		CODE GENERATOR				
	Compiler	Interpreter	Cobol	PL/1	Basic	Assembler	Other
				*			

EXECUTION MODE		OPERATION MODE	Batch	On-line	Multi-user
Under Product		Product	*	*	*
Independently	*	Application	*	*	*

SCOPE/ METHOD		DEFINITION OF:			
		Screens	Data	Processing	Reports
BY:	Screen Painting				
	Form Filling				
	Questionnaire				
	Commands	*	*	*	*

DEVELOPMENT ENVIRONMENT	OPTIONS				
INVOKED BY:	Menus		Commands		Other
FACILITIES	Help	S/R Screens	Editors	Debugging	Other Utilities
INTERFACE TO:	DBMS		TPM		Other Software *

PRICE/TERMS   From £6,800 to £23,000

INSTALLATIONS	NUMBER	FROM	TO
WORLD-WIDE	160	1/01/76	31/07/82
IN UK	11	1/06/81	31/12/82

DESCRIPTION: An application generator producing COBOL or PL/1. It supports a number of software engineering techniques including reusable code, data structured design methods, structured coding, etc. It improves development productivity by reducing time scales, improving quality and easing maintenance.

NAME ELIAS	VENDOR IBM

H/W IBM	OS VSE VM	TPM CICS CMS	OTHER COBOL or PL/1

TYPE	TRANSLATOR		CODE GENERATOR				
	Compiler	Interpreter	Cobol	PL/1	Basic	Assembler	Other
			*	*			*

EXECUTION MODE			OPERATION MODE	Batch	On-line	Multi-user
Under Product			Product		*	
Independently	*		Application	*	*	

SCOPE/ METHOD		DEFINITION OF:			
		Screens	Data	Processing	Reports
BY:	Screen Painting				
	Form Filling	*	*		
	Questionnaire				
	Commands				

DEVELOPMENT ENVIRONMENT	OPTIONS				
INVOKED BY:	Menus *		Commands		Other
FACILITIES	Help *	S/R Screens	Editors *	Debugging	Other Utilities
INTERFACE TO:	DBMS *		TPM *		Other Software *

PRICE/TERMS On application

INSTALLATIONS	NUMBER	FROM	TO
WORLD-WIDE			
IN UK			

DESCRIPTION: An interactive product designed to increase the productivity and simplify the tasks of designers and programmers who are implementing database or data comms applications with CICS/DOS/VS and/or DL/1 DOS/VS, using COBOL or PL/1. It is designed to support and extend both the VSE and VM/SP SIPOs with ELIAS-1 and ELIAS-1/VM.

NAME FACTORY	VENDOR CORTEX

H/W DEC VAX	OS VMS	TPM	OTHER APPLICATION

TYPE	TRANSLATOR		CODE GENERATOR				
	Compiler	Interpreter	Cobol	PL/1	Basic	Assembler	Other
		*					

EXECUTION MODE			OPERATION MODE	Batch	On-line	Multi-user
Under Product	*		Product		*	*
Independently			Application		*	*

SCOPE/ METHOD		DEFINITION OF:			
		Screens	Data	Processing	Reports
BY:	Screen Painting				
	Form Filling				
	Questionnaire	*	*		*
	Commands			*	

DEVELOPMENT ENVIRONMENT	OPTIONS				
INVOKED BY:	Menus		Commands		Other
FACILITIES	Help	S/R Screens	Editors	Debugging	Other Utilities
INTERFACE TO:	DBMS		TPM		Other Software *

PRICE/TERMS $15,000

INSTALLATIONS	NUMBER	FROM	TO
WORLD-WIDE	100	1/11/77	31/12/82
IN UK			

DESCRIPTION: Application generator.

NAME FILETAB	VENDOR NCC

H/W PORTABLE	OS VARIOUS	TPM VARIOUS	OTHER

TYPE	TRANSLATOR		CODE GENERATOR				
	Compiler	Interpreter	Cobol	PL/1	Basic	Assembler	Other
		*					

EXECUTION MODE		OPERATION MODE	Batch	On-line	Multi-user
Under Product	*	Product	*		
Independently		Application	*		

SCOPE/ METHOD		DEFINITION OF:			
		Screens	Data	Processing	Reports
BY:	Screen Painting				
	Form Filling				
	Questionnaire				
	Commands		*	*	*

DEVELOPMENT ENVIRONMENT	OPTIONS				
INVOKED BY:	Menus		Commands		Other
FACILITIES	Help	S/R Screens	Editors	Debugging	Other Utilities
INTERFACE TO:	DBMS		TPM *		Other Software *

PRICE/TERMS   On application

INSTALLATIONS	NUMBER	FROM	TO
WORLD-WIDE	350	1/01/71	31/12/82
IN UK	1000	1/01/69	31/12/82

DESCRIPTION: Reporting/File maintenance/File updating/Systems maintenance.

NAME	FMS-80	VENDOR	INFODATA

H/W	MICRO	OS	CP/M	TPM		OTHER	

TYPE	TRANSLATOR		CODE GENERATOR				
	Compiler	Interpreter	Cobol	PL/1	Basic	Assembler	Other
		*					

EXECUTION MODE		OPERATION MODE	Batch	On-line	Multi-user
Under Product	*	Product		*	*
Independently		Application		*	*

SCOPE/ METHOD		DEFINITION OF:			
		Screens	Data	Processing	Reports
BY:	Screen Painting	*	*		
	Form Filling	*	*		*
	Questionnaire				
	Commands			*	

DEVELOPMENT ENVIRONMENT	OPTIONS				
INVOKED BY:	Menus *		Commands		Other
FACILITIES	Help *	S/R Screens *	Editors *	Debugging *	Other Utilities *
INTERFACE TO:	DBMS		TPM		Other Software *

PRICE/TERMS	On application

INSTALLATIONS	NUMBER	FROM	TO
WORLD-WIDE			
IN UK			

DESCRIPTION: A powerful and general purpose File Management System for 8080 and Z80 based microcomputers.

NAME FOCUS	VENDOR INFOBUILD

H/W IBM	OS MVS VM	TPM VARIOUS	OTHER VARIOUS

TYPE	TRANSLATOR		CODE GENERATOR				
	Compiler	Interpreter	Cobol	PL/1	Basic	Assembler	Other
		*					

EXECUTION MODE		OPERATION MODE	Batch	On-line	Multi-user
Under Product	*	Product	*	*	*
Independently		Application	*	*	*

SCOPE/ METHOD		DEFINITION OF:			
		Screens	Data	Processing	Reports
BY:	Screen Painting				
	Form Filling	*	*	*	*
	Questionnaire	*	*	*	*
	Commands	*	*	*	*

DEVELOPMENT ENVIRONMENT	OPTIONS				
INVOKED BY:	Menus		Commands		Other *
FACILITIES	Help *	S/R Screens	Editors *	Debugging *	Other Utilities *
INTERFACE TO:	DBMS *		TPM *		Other Software *

PRICE/TERMS	From £26,300 to £71,000

INSTALLATIONS	NUMBER	FROM	TO
WORLD-WIDE	600	1/01/81	31/12/82
IN UK	32	1/01/81	31/12/82

DESCRIPTION: Information control system (IBMS) high-level, user-friendly, English-language commands for data retrieval and maintenance.

NAME GENERATION 5	VENDOR DATASOLVE

H/W IBM	OS MVS DOS OS	TPM	OTHER

TYPE	TRANSLATOR		CODE GENERATOR				
	Compiler	Interpreter	Cobol	PL/1	Basic	Assembler	Other
		*					

EXECUTION MODE			OPERATION MODE	Batch	On-line	Multi-user
Under Product	*		Product			
Independently			Application			

SCOPE/ METHOD		DEFINITION OF:			
		Screens	Data	Processing	Reports
BY:	Screen Painting				
	Form Filling				
	Questionnaire				
	Commands				

DEVELOPMENT ENVIRONMENT	OPTIONS				
INVOKED BY:	Menus		Commands		Other
FACILITIES	Help	S/R Screens	Editors	Debugging	Other Utilities
INTERFACE TO:	DBMS		TPM		Other Software

PRICE/TERMS On application

INSTALLATIONS	NUMBER	FROM	TO
WORLD-WIDE			
IN UK			

DESCRIPTION: Financial Application Program Generator (Vendor World-wide: American Management Systems U.S.A.)

PRODUCT SUMMARY DETAILS

NAME GRASS/34	VENDOR PRESTEDGE

H/W IBM SYSTEM 34	OS SSP	TPM	OTHER RPG 2

TYPE	TRANSLATOR		CODE GENERATOR				
	Compiler	Interpreter	Cobol	PL/1	Basic	Assembler	Other
							*

EXECUTION MODE		OPERATION MODE	Batch	On-line	Multi-user
Under Product		Product		*	*
Independently	*	Application		*	*

SCOPE/ METHOD		DEFINITION OF:			
		Screens	Data	Processing	Reports
BY:	Screen Painting				
	Form Filling				
	Questionnaire	*	*		*
	Commands				

DEVELOPMENT ENVIRONMENT	OPTIONS				
INVOKED BY:	Menus *		Commands		Other
FACILITIES	Help	S/R Screens	Editors	Debugging	Other Utilities
INTERFACE TO:	DBMS		TPM		Other Software

PRICE/TERMS £1,500

INSTALLATIONS	NUMBER	FROM	TO
WORLD-WIDE			
IN UK	5	1/09/82	10/12/82

DESCRIPTION: An application software generator for the IBM System 34. It consists of two RPG-2 program generators: one for screen validation programs and one for reports. They use a common data dictionary from which system documentation may also be obtained.

NAME GRS	VENDOR SYSCOM

H/W DEC	OS RSTS VMS	TPM	OTHER

TYPE	TRANSLATOR		CODE GENERATOR				
	Compiler	Interpreter	Cobol	PL/1	Basic	Assembler	Other
		*					

EXECUTION MODE			OPERATION MODE	Batch	On-line	Multi-user
Under Product	*		Product	*	*	*
Independently			Application	*	*	*

SCOPE/ METHOD		DEFINITION OF:			
		Screens	Data	Processing	Reports
BY:	Screen Painting				
	Form Filling				
	Questionnaire				
	Commands			*	*

DEVELOPMENT ENVIRONMENT	OPTIONS				
INVOKED BY:	Menus		Commands		Other
FACILITIES	Help	S/R Screens	Editors	Debugging	Other Utilities
INTERFACE TO:	DBMS		TPM		Other Software *

PRICE/TERMS	$4,800

INSTALLATIONS	NUMBER	FROM	TO
WORLD-WIDE	35	3/01/81	15/12/82
IN UK	6	15/08/81	1/11/82

DESCRIPTION: Query and report generation facility.

NAME	HLC	VENDOR	S+PC

H/W	MAINFRAME	OS	VARIOUS	TPM		OTHER	COBOL

TYPE	TRANSLATOR		CODE GENERATOR				
	Compiler	Interpreter	Cobol	PL/1	Basic	Assembler	Other
			*				

EXECUTION MODE		OPERATION MODE	Batch	On-line	Multi-user
Under Product		Product	*	*	*
Independently	*	Application	*	*	*

SCOPE/ METHOD		DEFINITION OF:			
		Screens	Data	Processing	Reports
BY:	Screen Painting				
	Form Filling				
	Questionnaire				
	Commands	*	*	*	*

DEVELOPMENT ENVIRONMENT	OPTIONS				
INVOKED BY:	Menus		Commands		Other
FACILITIES	Help	S/R Screens	Editors	Debugging	Other Utilities
INTERFACE TO:	DBMS		TPM		Other Software

PRICE/TERMS	From £2,615

INSTALLATIONS	NUMBER	FROM	TO
WORLD-WIDE	20	1/01/78	31/12/82
IN UK	35	1/01/76	31/12/82

DESCRIPTION: A Cobol code generator.

NAME	IDEAL	VENDOR	ADR

H/W	IBM	OS	ALL	TPM	CICS+	OTHER	DATACOM/DD

TYPE	TRANSLATOR		CODE GENERATOR				
	Compiler	Interpreter	Cobol	PL/1	Basic	Assembler	Other
	*	*					

EXECUTION MODE		OPERATION MODE	Batch	On-line	Multi-user
Under Product	*	Product		*	*
Independently		Application	*	*	*

SCOPE/ METHOD		DEFINITION OF:			
		Screens	Data	Processing	Reports
BY:	Screen Painting	*			*
	Form Filling	*	*		*
	Questionnaire				
	Commands			*	

DEVELOPMENT ENVIRONMENT	OPTIONS				
INVOKED BY:	Menus *		Commands		Other *
FACILITIES	Help *	S/R Screens *	Editors *	Debugging *	Other Utilities *
INTERFACE TO:	DBMS *		TPM *		Other Software *

PRICE/TERMS	On application

INSTALLATIONS	NUMBER	FROM	TO
WORLD-WIDE			
IN UK			

DESCRIPTION: NEW PRODUCT – An interactive application development and execution system with its own automated development support environment. It integrates a fully active data dictionary, relational DBMS and a fourth generation non-procedural language in a single, user-friendly environment.

NAME INFO	**VENDOR** DORIC

H/W PORTABLE	**OS** VARIOUS	**TPM**	**OTHER**

TYPE	TRANSLATOR		CODE GENERATOR				
	Compiler	Interpreter	Cobol	PL/1	Basic	Assembler	Other
		*					

EXECUTION MODE		**OPERATION MODE**	Batch	On-line	Multi-user
Under Product	*	Product		*	*
Independently		Application	*	*	*

SCOPE/ METHOD		DEFINITION OF:			
		Screens	Data	Processing	Reports
BY:	Screen Painting	*			*
	Form Filling				
	Questionnaire				
	Commands		*	*	

DEVELOPMENT ENVIRONMENT	OPTIONS				
INVOKED BY:	Menus *		Commands		Other
FACILITIES	Help *	S/R Screens	Editors *	Debugging *	Other Utilities
INTERFACE TO:	DBMS *		TPM *		Other Software *

PRICE/TERMS   From £10,000 to £15,000

INSTALLATIONS	NUMBER	FROM	TO
WORLD-WIDE	800	1/01/75	31/12/82
IN UK	80	5/05/80	20/12/82

DESCRIPTION: A fourth generation language designed for use by both DP and end-user personnel as an on-line file enquiry and reporting tool or as a standard DP language for developing full applications. It is a uniquely columnar product in that it handles everything from disk input/output to complex programming of multi-user systems.

NAME	INSYST	VENDOR	CIRCLE

H/W	IBM	OS	DOS OS MVS	TPM	CICS	OTHER	

TYPE	TRANSLATOR		CODE GENERATOR				
	Compiler	Interpreter	Cobol	PL/1	Basic	Assembler	Other
		*					

EXECUTION MODE			OPERATION MODE	Batch	On-line	Multi-user
Under Product	*		Product		*	*
Independently			Application		*	*

SCOPE/ METHOD		DEFINITION OF:			
		Screens	Data	Processing	Reports
BY:	Screen Painting				
	Form Filling	*	*	*	
	Questionnaire				
	Commands				

DEVELOPMENT ENVIRONMENT	OPTIONS				
INVOKED BY:	Menus		Commands		Other *
FACILITIES	Help	S/R Screens	Editors	Debugging	Other Utilities
INTERFACE TO:	DBMS		TPM		Other Software

PRICE/TERMS	On application

INSTALLATIONS	NUMBER	FROM	TO
WORLD-WIDE	30	1/01/81	31/12/82
IN UK	10	1/01/81	31/12/82

DESCRIPTION: On-line system generator package.

NAME LINC	VENDOR BURROUGHS

H/W B1000-7000	OS	TPM	OTHER

TYPE	TRANSLATOR		CODE GENERATOR				
	Compiler	Interpreter	Cobol	PL/1	Basic	Assembler	Other
	*		*				

EXECUTION MODE		OPERATION MODE	Batch	On-line	Multi-user
Under Product	*	Product	*	*	*
Independently		Application	*	*	*

SCOPE/ METHOD		DEFINITION OF:			
		Screens	Data	Processing	Reports
BY:	Screen Painting	*			*
	Form Filling		*		
	Questionnaire				
	Commands			*	

DEVELOPMENT ENVIRONMENT	OPTIONS				
INVOKED BY:	Menus		Commands		Other
FACILITIES	Help	S/R Screens	Editors *	Debugging *	Other Utilities *
INTERFACE TO:	DBMS *		TPM *		Other Software *

PRICE/TERMS   From £34,000 to £115,000

INSTALLATIONS	NUMBER	FROM	TO
WORLD-WIDE	240	1/03/82	31/01/83
IN UK	24	1/06/82	31/01/83

DESCRIPTION: Application system generator.

NAME MANTIS	VENDOR CINCOM

H/W IBM	OS DOS OS MVS	TPM CICS	OTHER VSAM

TYPE	TRANSLATOR		CODE GENERATOR				
	Compiler	Interpreter	Cobol	PL/1	Basic	Assembler	Other
		*					

EXECUTION MODE			OPERATION MODE	Batch	On-line	Multi-user
Under Product	*		Product		*	*
Independently			Application		*	*

SCOPE/ METHOD		DEFINITION OF:			
		Screens	Data	Processing	Reports
BY:	Screen Painting	*			*
	Form Filling		*		
	Questionnaire				
	Commands	*		*	

DEVELOPMENT ENVIRONMENT	OPTIONS				
INVOKED BY:	Menus *		Commands		Other
FACILITIES	Help *	S/R Screens	Editors *	Debugging *	Other Utilities *
INTERFACE TO:	DBMS *		TPM *		Other Software *

PRICE/TERMS   On application

INSTALLATIONS	NUMBER	FROM	TO
WORLD-WIDE	700	1/04/81	31/12/82
IN UK	60	1/04/81	31/12/82

DESCRIPTION: Fourth generation application development system provides full on-line development capabilities, including complete interactive screen design, file design, logical view access to database or IBM standard access methods, programming and documentation.

NAME MAPPER	**VENDOR** SPERRY

H/W UNIVAC	**OS** OS/1100	**TPM**	**OTHER**

	TRANSLATOR		CODE GENERATOR				
TYPE	Compiler	Interpreter	Cobol	PL/1	Basic	Assembler	Other
		*					

EXECUTION MODE		**OPERATION MODE**	Batch	On-line	Multi-user
Under Product	*	Product		*	*
Independently		Application		*	*

SCOPE/ METHOD		DEFINITION OF:			
		Screens	Data	Processing	Reports
BY:	Screen Painting				
	Form Filling				
	Questionnaire				
	Commands	*	*	*	*

DEVELOPMENT ENVIRONMENT	OPTIONS				
INVOKED BY:	Menus		Commands		Other
FACILITIES	Help *	S/R Screens	Editors *	Debugging *	Other Utilities *
INTERFACE TO:	DBMS *		TPM *		Other Software

PRICE/TERMS   £985 per month

INSTALLATIONS	NUMBER	FROM	TO
WORLD-WIDE	530	1/04/79	31/12/82
IN UK	15	1/04/81	31/12/82

DESCRIPTION: Software for application development, report generation and data manipulation.

NAME MARK IV	VENDOR INFORMATICS

H/W IBM 370	OS DOS OS MVS	TPM IMS/DC	OTHER VARIOUS

TYPE	TRANSLATOR		CODE GENERATOR				
	Compiler	Interpreter	Cobol	PL/1	Basic	Assembler	Other
	*						*

EXECUTION MODE	
Under Product	
Independently	*

OPERATION MODE	Batch	On-line	Multi-user
Product	*		*
Application	*		*

SCOPE/ METHOD		DEFINITION OF:			
		Screens	Data	Processing	Reports
BY:	Screen Painting				
	Form Filling		*	*	*
	Questionnaire				
	Commands		*	*	*

DEVELOPMENT ENVIRONMENT	OPTIONS				
INVOKED BY:	Menus		Commands		Other
FACILITIES	Help	S/R Screens	Editors *	Debugging *	Other Utilities *
INTERFACE TO:	DBMS *		TPM *		Other Software *

PRICE/TERMS   On application

INSTALLATIONS	NUMBER	FROM	TO
WORLD-WIDE			
IN UK			

DESCRIPTION: A batch application generator.

NAME MARK V	**VENDOR** INFORMATICS

H/W IBM 370	**OS** OS DOS MVS	**TPM** IMS/DC	**OTHER** VARIOUS

TYPE	TRANSLATOR		CODE GENERATOR				
	Compiler	Interpreter	Cobol	PL/1	Basic	Assembler	Other
	*						*

EXECUTION MODE		OPERATION MODE	Batch	On-line	Multi-user
Under Product		Product	*	*	*
Independently	*	Application		*	*

SCOPE/ METHOD		DEFINITION OF:			
		Screens	Data	Processing	Reports
BY:	Screen Painting	*			
	Form Filling				
	Questionnaire				
	Commands	*	*	*	

DEVELOPMENT ENVIRONMENT	OPTIONS				
INVOKED BY:	Menus		Commands		Other *
FACILITIES	Help	S/R Screens *	Editors *	Debugging *	Other Utilities *
INTERFACE TO:	DBMS *		TPM *		Other Software *

PRICE/TERMS   On application

INSTALLATIONS	NUMBER	FROM	TO
WORLD-WIDE			
IN UK			

DESCRIPTION: IMS on-line application generator.

NAME MIMER	VENDOR SAVANT

H/W PORTABLE	OS VARIOUS	TPM VARIOUS	OTHER VARIOUS

TYPE	TRANSLATOR		CODE GENERATOR				
	Compiler	Interpreter	Cobol	PL/1	Basic	Assembler	Other
			*				*

EXECUTION MODE	
Under Product	
Independently	*

OPERATION MODE	Batch	On-line	Multi-user
Product		*	*
Application		*	*

SCOPE/ METHOD		DEFINITION OF:			
		Screens	Data	Processing	Reports
BY:	Screen Painting				
	Form Filling				
	Questionnaire				
	Commands	*	*	*	*

DEVELOPMENT ENVIRONMENT	OPTIONS				
INVOKED BY:	Menus		Commands		Other
FACILITIES	Help	S/R Screens	Editors	Debugging	Other Utilities
INTERFACE TO:	DBMS		TPM		Other Software

PRICE/TERMS   From £4,000 (micros) to £35,550 (mainframes)

INSTALLATIONS	NUMBER	FROM	TO
WORLD-WIDE	75	1/01/78	31/12/82
IN UK			

DESCRIPTION: A relational database management system with user-friendly query language, application and software generator, screen handler, information retrieval system and links to statistical and graphics packages.

NAME MIS/OL	**VENDOR** PANSOPHIC

H/W IBM	**OS** OS DOS	**TPM** CICS	**OTHER**

TYPE	TRANSLATOR		CODE GENERATOR				
	Compiler	Interpreter	Cobol	PL/1	Basic	Assembler	Other
			*	*			

EXECUTION MODE		**OPERATION MODE**	Batch	On-line	Multi-user
Under Product		Product		*	*
Independently	*	Application		*	*

SCOPE/ METHOD		DEFINITION OF:			
		Screens	Data	Processing	Reports
BY:	Screen Painting	*			
	Form Filling		*		
	Questionnaire				
	Commands				

DEVELOPMENT ENVIRONMENT	OPTIONS				
INVOKED BY:	Menus		Commands		Other
FACILITIES	Help	S/R Screens	Editors	Debugging	Other Utilities *
INTERFACE TO:	DBMS *		TPM *		Other Software *

PRICE/TERMS On request

INSTALLATIONS	NUMBER	FROM	TO
WORLD-WIDE	120	1/01/80	1/12/82
IN UK	6	1/11/82	1/12/82

DESCRIPTION: A comprehensive product created specifically to streamline applications development under CICS/VS.

NAME MM	VENDOR TSI

H/W IBM	OS VSE VS1 MVS	TPM CICS +	OTHER

TYPE	TRANSLATOR		CODE GENERATOR				
	Compiler	Interpreter	Cobol	PL/1	Basic	Assembler	Other

EXECUTION MODE		OPERATION MODE	Batch	On-line	Multi-user
Under Product	*	Product		*	*
Independently		Application		*	*

SCOPE/ METHOD		DEFINITION OF:			
		Screens	Data	Processing	Reports
BY:	Screen Painting				
	Form Filling	*			
	Questionnaire				
	Commands				

DEVELOPMENT ENVIRONMENT	OPTIONS		
INVOKED BY:	Menus	Commands	Other
FACILITIES	Help	S/R Screens	Editors *	Debugging *	Other Utilities
INTERFACE TO:	DBMS *	TPM *	Other Software *

PRICE/TERMS   From £7000

INSTALLATIONS	NUMBER	FROM	TO
WORLD-WIDE	200	1/01/75	31/12/82
IN UK			

DESCRIPTION: An on-line programmer productivity tool. It provides interactive screen format definition and testing facilities. Generated formats can be specified with a comprehensive range of edit checks that ensure that data passed to user-written application programs is completely valid.

NAME MUM	VENDOR FRETWELL

H/W MINI	OS VARIOUS	TPM	OTHER

TYPE	TRANSLATOR		CODE GENERATOR				
	Compiler	Interpreter	Cobol	PL/1	Basic	Assembler	Other
		*					

EXECUTION MODE		OPERATION MODE	Batch	On-line	Multi-user
Under Product	*	Product		*	*
Independently		Application		*	*

SCOPE/ METHOD		DEFINITION OF:			
		Screens	Data	Processing	Reports
BY:	Screen Painting				
	Form Filling	*	*	*	*
	Questionnaire				
	Commands				

DEVELOPMENT ENVIRONMENT	OPTIONS				
INVOKED BY:	Menus *		Commands		Other *
FACILITIES	Help	S/R Screens	Editors *	Debugging	Other Utilities
INTERFACE TO:	DBMS		TPM		Other Software *

PRICE/TERMS   From £9,000

INSTALLATIONS	NUMBER	FROM	TO
WORLD-WIDE			
IN UK	16	1/08/81	1/12/82

DESCRIPTION: Portable self-contained parameter programming environment for developing machine independent solutions to information management problems.

NAME NATURAL	VENDOR ADABAS

H/W IBM	OS ALL	TPM CICS+	OTHER ADABAS DBMS

TYPE	TRANSLATOR		CODE GENERATOR				
	Compiler	Interpreter	Cobol	PL/1	Basic	Assembler	Other
	*						

EXECUTION MODE			OPERATION MODE		Batch	On-line	Multi-user
Under Product	*		Product		*	*	*
Independently			Application		*	*	*

SCOPE/ METHOD		DEFINITION OF:			
		Screens	Data	Processing	Reports
BY:	Screen Painting				
	Form Filling	*	*		*
	Questionnaire				
	Commands			*	

DEVELOPMENT ENVIRONMENT	OPTIONS				
INVOKED BY:	Menus		Commands		Other
FACILITIES	Help *	S/R Screens	Editors *	Debugging *	Other Utilities *
INTERFACE TO:	DBMS *		TPM *		Other Software

PRICE/TERMS From £20,000 (DOS) or rental £450 /month over 5 yrs

INSTALLATIONS	NUMBER	FROM	TO
WORLD-WIDE	950	1/01/79	31/12/82
IN UK	45	1/01/79	31/12/82

DESCRIPTION: An on-line and batch programming language, enquiry, report writer and end-user facility – for use with ADABAS DBMS, VSAM and sequential files – complete with screen painting, multi-screen support, and self contained program development and library facilities.

NAME NUCLEUS	VENDOR COMPACT

H/W MICRO	OS CP/M	TPM	OTHER MBASIC

TYPE	TRANSLATOR		CODE GENERATOR				
	Compiler	Interpreter	Cobol	PL/1	Basic	Assembler	Other
					*		

EXECUTION MODE		OPERATION MODE	Batch	On-line	Multi-user
Under Product		Product		*	
Independently	*	Application		*	

SCOPE/ METHOD		DEFINITION OF:			
		Screens	Data	Processing	Reports
BY:	Screen Painting				
	Form Filling				
	Questionnaire	*	*	*	*
	Commands				

DEVELOPMENT ENVIRONMENT	OPTIONS				
INVOKED BY:	Menus *		Commands		Other
FACILITIES	Help	S/R Screens	Editors	Debugging	Other Utilities
INTERFACE TO:	DBMS		TPM		Other Software *

PRICE/TERMS £990

INSTALLATIONS	NUMBER	FROM	TO
WORLD-WIDE	520	1/01/82	31/12/82
IN UK			

DESCRIPTION: System and report generator creating MBASIC programs. Note: UK Installations bundled into world-wide figures.

NAME OLGEN	VENDOR WATSONS

H/W BURROUGHS	OS MCP	TPM	OTHER COBOL

TYPE	TRANSLATOR		CODE GENERATOR				
	Compiler	Interpreter	Cobol	PL/1	Basic	Assembler	Other
	*		*				

EXECUTION MODE		OPERATION MODE	Batch	On-line	Multi-user
Under Product		Product		*	*
Independently	*	Application		*	*

SCOPE/ METHOD		DEFINITION OF:			
		Screens	Data	Processing	Reports
BY:	Screen Painting				
	Form Filling	*	*		*
	Questionnaire		*		*
	Commands				

DEVELOPMENT ENVIRONMENT	OPTIONS				
INVOKED BY:	Menus *		Commands		Other
FACILITIES	Help *	S/R Screens	Editors *	Debugging	Other Utilities
INTERFACE TO:	DBMS		TPM		Other Software

PRICE/TERMS On application

INSTALLATIONS	NUMBER	FROM	TO
WORLD-WIDE	5	1/09/82	1/12/82
IN UK	15	1/06/81	8/08/82

DESCRIPTION: A generator of applications to maintain, enquire, report and update database structures.

NAME	ORACLE (1)	VENDOR	DATAB

H/W	ICL	OS	TME DME	TPM	BITOS	OTHER	ISAM

TYPE	TRANSLATOR		CODE GENERATOR				
	Compiler	Interpreter	Cobol	PL/1	Basic	Assembler	Other
		*					

EXECUTION MODE		OPERATION MODE	Batch	On-line	Multi-user
Under Product	*	Product		*	*
Independently		Application		*	*

SCOPE/ METHOD		DEFINITION OF:			
		Screens	Data	Processing	Reports
BY:	Screen Painting	*			
	Form Filling	*			
	Questionnaire				
	Commands		*	*	

DEVELOPMENT ENVIRONMENT	OPTIONS				
INVOKED BY:	Menus *		Commands		Other
FACILITIES	Help	S/R Screens	Editors	Debugging	Other Utilities
INTERFACE TO:	DBMS		TPM *		Other Software *

PRICE/TERMS	£3,000

INSTALLATIONS	NUMBER	FROM	TO
WORLD-WIDE			
IN UK			

DESCRIPTION: An on-line enquiry system generator. (New product).

NAME ORACLE (2)	VENDOR CACI

H/W DEC	OS	TPM	OTHER

TYPE	TRANSLATOR		CODE GENERATOR				
	Compiler	Interpreter	Cobol	PL/1	Basic	Assembler	Other
		*					

EXECUTION MODE			OPERATION MODE	Batch	On-line	Multi-user
Under Product	*		Product		*	*
Independently			Application		*	*

SCOPE/ METHOD		DEFINITION OF:			
		Screens	Data	Processing	Reports
BY:	Screen Painting	*			
	Form Filling				
	Questionnaire				
	Commands	*	*	*	*

DEVELOPMENT ENVIRONMENT	OPTIONS				
INVOKED BY:	Menus *		Commands		Other
FACILITIES	Help *	S/R Screens	Editors *	Debugging *	Other Utilities
INTERFACE TO:	DBMS *		TPM *		Other Software *

PRICE/TERMS   On application

INSTALLATIONS	NUMBER	FROM	TO
WORLD-WIDE	210	1/07/79	13/12/82
IN UK			

DESCRIPTION: The interactive application facility enables screens to be specified and painted and allows data to be inserted, updated or deleted. The product includes a relational database. It will be available on IBM from early 1983.

NAME PACT	VENDOR THREE-D

H/W IBM	OS VS	TPM	OTHER COBOL or PL/1

TYPE	TRANSLATOR		CODE GENERATOR				
	Compiler	Interpreter	Cobol	PL/1	Basic	Assembler	Other
			*	*			

EXECUTION MODE			OPERATION MODE	Batch	On-line	Multi-user
Under Product			Product	*	*	
Independently	*		Application	*		

SCOPE/ METHOD		DEFINITION OF:			
		Screens	Data	Processing	Reports
BY:	Screen Painting				
	Form Filling				
	Questionnaire				
	Commands		*		*

DEVELOPMENT ENVIRONMENT	OPTIONS				
INVOKED BY:	Menus		Commands		Other
FACILITIES	Help	S/R Screens	Editors	Debugging	Other Utilities
INTERFACE TO:	DBMS		TPM		Other Software

PRICE/TERMS £4,900

INSTALLATIONS	NUMBER	FROM	TO
WORLD-WIDE			
IN UK	1		31/12/82

DESCRIPTION: Purpose is to translate a program designed in the Michael Jackson style into compilable PL/1, Assembler or Cobol for IBM hardware.

NAME PANEL	VENDOR ROUNDHILL

H/W MICRO	OS CP/M MS-DOS	TPM	OTHER

TYPE	TRANSLATOR		CODE GENERATOR				
	Compiler	Interpreter	Cobol	PL/1	Basic	Assembler	Other
			*	*			*

EXECUTION MODE		OPERATION MODE	Batch	On-line	Multi-user
Under Product		Product		*	
Independently	*	Application		*	

SCOPE/ METHOD		DEFINITION OF:			
		Screens	Data	Processing	Reports
BY:	Screen Painting	*			
	Form Filling		*		
	Questionnaire				
	Commands				

DEVELOPMENT ENVIRONMENT	OPTIONS				
INVOKED BY:	Menus		Commands		Other
FACILITIES	Help	S/R Screens	Editors	Debugging	Other Utilities
INTERFACE TO:	DBMS		TPM		Other Software *

PRICE/TERMS $380 (UK price)

INSTALLATIONS	NUMBER	FROM	TO
WORLD-WIDE	25	1/07/81	31/12/82
IN UK	75	1/04/81	31/12/82

DESCRIPTION: An application development tool which allows screen layouts to be set up and modified interactively. The system either generates code for inclusion in an application program or can access screen layouts at run time. Applications can be run on any screen type without change.

NAME PER PEARL	**VENDOR** PEARL

H/W MICRO	**OS** CP/M	**TPM**	**OTHER**

TYPE	TRANSLATOR		CODE GENERATOR				
	Compiler	Interpreter	Cobol	PL/1	Basic	Assembler	Other
		*					

EXECUTION MODE	
Under Product	*
Independently	

OPERATION MODE	Batch	On-line	Multi-user
Product		*	
Application		*	

SCOPE/ METHOD		DEFINITION OF:			
		Screens	Data	Processing	Reports
BY:	Screen Painting	*			*
	Form Filling		*		
	Questionnaire				
	Commands				

DEVELOPMENT ENVIRONMENT	OPTIONS				
INVOKED BY:	Menus *	Commands		Other	
FACILITIES	Help *	S/R Screens	Editors *	Debugging	Other Utilities
INTERFACE TO:	DBMS	TPM		Other Software	

PRICE/TERMS $295 (US price)

INSTALLATIONS	NUMBER	FROM	TO
WORLD-WIDE			
IN UK			

DESCRIPTION: Relational database and program generator engineered for end-users who wish to design their own customised software. Interfaces with spreadsheet and WP for additional product flexibility.

NAME PRELUDE	VENDOR CORES

H/W MINIS	OS PICK	TPM	OTHER

TYPE	TRANSLATOR		CODE GENERATOR				
	Compiler	Interpreter	Cobol	PL/1	Basic	Assembler	Other
					*		

EXECUTION MODE			OPERATION MODE	Batch	On-line	Multi-user
Under Product	*		Product		*	*
Independently			Application		*	*

SCOPE/ METHOD		DEFINITION OF:			
		Screens	Data	Processing	Reports
BY:	Screen Painting	*			*
	Form Filling				
	Questionnaire				
	Commands		*	*	

DEVELOPMENT ENVIRONMENT	OPTIONS				
INVOKED BY:	Menus *		Commands		Other
FACILITIES	Help	S/R Screens	Editors	Debugging	Other Utilities
INTERFACE TO:	DBMS		TPM		Other Software

PRICE/TERMS Bundled in hardware purchased from vendor.

INSTALLATIONS	NUMBER	FROM	TO
WORLD-WIDE			
IN UK	1	1/07/82	31/12/82

DESCRIPTION: System generator.

NAME PRIDE	VENDOR MBA

H/W PORTABLE	OS VARIOUS	TPM VARIOUS	OTHER VARIOUS

TYPE	TRANSLATOR		CODE GENERATOR				
	Compiler	Interpreter	Cobol	PL/1	Basic	Assembler	Other
			*	*			

EXECUTION MODE		OPERATION MODE	Batch	On-line	Multi-user
Under Product		Product		*	*
Independently	*	Application	*	*	*

SCOPE/ METHOD		DEFINITION OF:			
		Screens	Data	Processing	Reports
BY:	Screen Painting				
	Form Filling				
	Questionnaire	*	*	*	*
	Commands				

DEVELOPMENT ENVIRONMENT	OPTIONS		
INVOKED BY:	Menus *	Commands	Other
FACILITIES	Help *	S/R Screens	Editors *	Debugging	Other Utilities
INTERFACE TO:	DBMS	TPM	Other Software

PRICE/TERMS $80,000 (US price)

INSTALLATIONS	NUMBER	FROM	TO
WORLD-WIDE	1000	1/01/71	31/12/82
IN UK	2	1/01/76	31/12/82

DESCRIPTION: An Automated System Design Methodology which is a pragmatic, comprehensive approach for controlling an organisations systems development activities.

NAME PRO/GRAMMAR	VENDOR PANSOPHIC

H/W IBM	OS VM OS DOS	TPM	OTHER VARIOUS

TYPE	TRANSLATOR		CODE GENERATOR				
	Compiler	Interpreter	Cobol	PL/1	Basic	Assembler	Other
	*	*					

EXECUTION MODE	
Under Product	*
Independently	

OPERATION MODE	Batch	On-line	Multi-user
Product	*		
Application	*		*

SCOPE/ METHOD		DEFINITION OF:			
		Screens	Data	Processing	Reports
BY:	Screen Painting				
	Form Filling				
	Questionnaire				
	Commands		*	*	*

DEVELOPMENT ENVIRONMENT	OPTIONS				
INVOKED BY:	Menus		Commands		Other
FACILITIES	Help	S/R Screens	Editors	Debugging	Other Utilities
INTERFACE TO:	DBMS *		TPM		Other Software *

PRICE/TERMS On application

INSTALLATIONS	NUMBER	FROM	TO
WORLD-WIDE	110	1/01/82	1/12/82
IN UK	10	1/01/82	1/12/82

DESCRIPTION: An information retrieval and applications development system. It is a general purpose productivity aid for the design, development, implementation and operation of DP applications.

NAME PROGAPP	VENDOR LIFEBOAT

H/W MICRO	OS CP/M	TPM	OTHER MBASIC

TYPE	TRANSLATOR		CODE GENERATOR				
	Compiler	Interpreter	Cobol	PL/1	Basic	Assembler	Other
					*		

EXECUTION MODE			OPERATION MODE	Batch	On-line	Multi-user
Under Product			Product		*	
Independently	*		Application		*	

SCOPE/ METHOD		DEFINITION OF:			
		Screens	Data	Processing	Reports
BY:	Screen Painting	*			*
	Form Filling		*		
	Questionnaire				
	Commands			*	

DEVELOPMENT ENVIRONMENT	OPTIONS				
INVOKED BY:	Menus *		Commands		Other
FACILITIES	Help *	S/R Screens	Editors *	Debugging *	Other Utilities
INTERFACE TO:	DBMS		TPM		Other Software

PRICE/TERMS £485

INSTALLATIONS	NUMBER	FROM	TO
WORLD-WIDE			
IN UK			

DESCRIPTION: Program development tool.

APPLICATION PROGRAM GENERATORS

NAME	PROMACS	VENDOR	MACS

H/W	IBM	OS	DOS OS VM	TPM	VARIOUS	OTHER	VARIOUS

	TRANSLATOR		CODE GENERATOR				
TYPE	Compiler	Interpreter	Cobol	PL/1	Basic	Assembler	Other
			*				

EXECUTION MODE	
Under Product	
Independently	*

OPERATION MODE	Batch	On-line	Multi-user
Product		*	
Application	*	*	*

SCOPE/ METHOD		DEFINITION OF:			
		Screens	Data	Processing	Reports
BY:	Screen Painting				
	Form Filling				
	Questionnaire				
	Commands	*	*	*	*

DEVELOPMENT ENVIRONMENT	OPTIONS				
INVOKED BY:	Menus		Commands		Other
FACILITIES	Help	S/R Screens	Editors	Debugging	Other Utilities
INTERFACE TO:	DBMS *		TPM *		Other Software *

PRICE/TERMS	From $18,000 (US price)

INSTALLATIONS	NUMBER	FROM	TO
WORLD-WIDE	60	1/01/79	31/12/82
IN UK			

DESCRIPTION: A free-form, high-level, non-procedural programming system similar in syntax to COBOL, but much more concise, more powerful and easier to use.

NAME RAMIS	VENDOR MATHEMATICA

H/W IBM	OS VS MVS VSE	TPM VARIOUS	OTHER VARIOUS

TYPE	TRANSLATOR		CODE GENERATOR				
	Compiler	Interpreter	Cobol	PL/1	Basic	Assembler	Other
		*					

EXECUTION MODE		OPERATION MODE	Batch	On-line	Multi-user
Under Product	*	Product	*	*	
Independently		Application	*	*	

SCOPE/ METHOD		DEFINITION OF:			
		Screens	Data	Processing	Reports
BY:	Screen Painting	*			
	Form Filling	*	*		
	Questionnaire				
	Commands	*	*	*	*

DEVELOPMENT ENVIRONMENT	OPTIONS				
INVOKED BY:	Menus		Commands		Other
FACILITIES	Help *	S/R Screens	Editors *	Debugging *	Other Utilities *
INTERFACE TO:	DBMS *		TPM *		Other Software *

PRICE/TERMS   On application

INSTALLATIONS	NUMBER	FROM	TO
WORLD-WIDE	836	1/01/75	31/12/82
IN UK	75	1/01/75	31/12/82

DESCRIPTION: A fourth generation language comprising a database manager, non-procedural reporting language, non-procedural data maintenance language, application development environment, plus editors, screen management facilities and business graphics.

NAME RAPID	VENDOR HP

H/W HP 3000	OS	TPM	OTHER

TYPE	TRANSLATOR		CODE GENERATOR				
	Compiler	Interpreter	Cobol	PL/1	Basic	Assembler	Other
		*					

EXECUTION MODE		OPERATION MODE	Batch	On-line	Multi-user
Under Product	*	Product		*	*
Independently		Application		*	*

SCOPE/ METHOD		DEFINITION OF:			
		Screens	Data	Processing	Reports
BY:	Screen Painting				
	Form Filling	*	*		
	Questionnaire				
	Commands			*	*

DEVELOPMENT ENVIRONMENT	OPTIONS				
INVOKED BY:	Menus *		Commands		Other
FACILITIES	Help *	S/R Screens	Editors *	Debugging *	Other Utilities *
INTERFACE TO:	DBMS		TPM		Other Software *

PRICE/TERMS   From £7,000

INSTALLATIONS	NUMBER	FROM	TO
WORLD-WIDE			
IN UK	50	1/01/82	31/12/82

DESCRIPTION: A data dictionary approach to referencing and documenting data held in database/files/graphs/forms with enquiry facilities (INFORM + REPORT) together with a high-level transaction (TRANSACT) processing language. The product consists of four components, DICTIONARY, TRANSACT, INFORM and REPORT.

NAME RDM	VENDOR UNIT-C

H/W DEC PDP-11	OS	TPM	OTHER

TYPE	TRANSLATOR		CODE GENERATOR				
	Compiler	Interpreter	Cobol	PL/1	Basic	Assembler	Other
		*					

EXECUTION MODE		OPERATION MODE	Batch	On-line	Multi-user
Under Product	*	Product		*	*
Independently		Application		*	*

SCOPE/ METHOD		DEFINITION OF:			
		Screens	Data	Processing	Reports
BY:	Screen Painting				
	Form Filling				
	Questionnaire				
	Commands				

DEVELOPMENT ENVIRONMENT	OPTIONS				
INVOKED BY:	Menus		Commands		Other
FACILITIES	Help	S/R Screens	Editors	Debugging	Other Utilities
INTERFACE TO:	DBMS		TPM		Other Software

PRICE/TERMS $2500 (US price)

INSTALLATIONS	NUMBER	FROM	TO
WORLD-WIDE	110		30/09/82
IN UK	1		31/12/82

DESCRIPTION: Application development software without writing code. General purpose.

NAME READYCODE	VENDOR DATA LOGIC

H/W IBM	OS VARIOUS	TPM VARIOUS	OTHER COBOL

TYPE	TRANSLATOR		CODE GENERATOR				
	Compiler	Interpreter	Cobol	PL/1	Basic	Assembler	Other
			*				

EXECUTION MODE	
Under Product	
Independently	*

OPERATION MODE	Batch	On-line	Multi-user
Product	*	*	*
Application	*	*	*

SCOPE/ METHOD		DEFINITION OF:			
		Screens	Data	Processing	Reports
BY:	Screen Painting	*			*
	Form Filling	*	*		*
	Questionnaire				
	Commands				

DEVELOPMENT ENVIRONMENT	OPTIONS				
INVOKED BY:	Menus *		Commands		Other *
FACILITIES	Help *	S/R Screens	Editors *	Debugging *	Other Utilities *
INTERFACE TO:	DBMS *		TPM *		Other Software *

PRICE/TERMS   From £30,000

INSTALLATIONS	NUMBER	FROM	TO
WORLD-WIDE			
IN UK	1	1/09/82	31/12/82

DESCRIPTION: An application program generator system that significantly reduces COBOL programs development, testing and maintenance. Two major components – SDS, generates COBOL programs and SMS, monitors and indexes the development system. Uses pre-tested logic, re-usable code and embedded documentation.

NAME	SILICON OFF	VENDOR	BSF

H/W	MICROS	OS	TPM	OTHER

TYPE	TRANSLATOR		CODE GENERATOR				
	Compiler	Interpreter	Cobol	PL/1	Basic	Assembler	Other
		*					

EXECUTION MODE		OPERATION MODE	Batch	On-line	Multi-user
Under Product	*	Product		*	
Independently		Application		*	

SCOPE/ METHOD		DEFINITION OF:			
		Screens	Data	Processing	Reports
BY:	Screen Painting				
	Form Filling				
	Questionnaire				
	Commands	*	*	*	*

DEVELOPMENT ENVIRONMENT	OPTIONS				
INVOKED BY:	Menus *		Commands		Other
FACILITIES	Help *	S/R Screens	Editors *	Debugging *	Other Utilities *
INTERFACE TO:	DBMS		TPM		Other Software *

PRICE/TERMS	£790 ex VAT

INSTALLATIONS	NUMBER	FROM	TO
WORLD-WIDE	1400	1/10/81	31/12/82
IN UK	2200	1/10/81	31/12/82

DESCRIPTION: Database management system and word processor integrated to provide an applications generator. Mk 1 version for DBM 8096. Mk 2 version for Sirius, Victor and mid-1983 for IBM and DEC PC.

NAME SOFTOOL	VENDOR SOFTOOL

H/W VARIOUS	OS VARIOUS	TPM	OTHER FORTRAN

TYPE	TRANSLATOR		CODE GENERATOR				
	Compiler	Interpreter	Cobol	PL/1	Basic	Assembler	Other
							*

EXECUTION MODE			OPERATION MODE	Batch	On-line	Multi-user
Under Product			Product		*	*
Independently	*		Application		*	*

SCOPE/ METHOD		DEFINITION OF:			
		Screens	Data	Processing	Reports
BY:	Screen Painting				
	Form Filling				
	Questionnaire				
	Commands				

DEVELOPMENT ENVIRONMENT	OPTIONS				
INVOKED BY:	Menus		Commands		Other
FACILITIES	Help	S/R Screens	Editors	Debugging	Other Utilities
INTERFACE TO:	DBMS		TPM		Other Software

PRICE/TERMS $60,000 (US price)

INSTALLATIONS	NUMBER	FROM	TO
WORLD-WIDE	750	1/01/80	31/12/82
IN UK	1		31/12/82

DESCRIPTION: Programming environment. The user comes with a design document and leaves with a completed software product including source and object code, extensive documentation, test reports, optimisation reports, etc.

NAME SQL/DS	VENDOR IBM

H/W IBM	OS VSE	TPM IMS/DC	OTHER

TYPE	TRANSLATOR		CODE GENERATOR				
	Compiler	Interpreter	Cobol	PL/1	Basic	Assembler	Other
	*						

EXECUTION MODE		OPERATION MODE	Batch	On-line	Multi-user
Under Product	*	Product	*	*	*
Independently		Application	*	*	*

SCOPE/ METHOD		DEFINITION OF:			
		Screens	Data	Processing	Reports
BY:	Screen Painting				
	Form Filling				
	Questionnaire				
	Commands		*	*	*

DEVELOPMENT ENVIRONMENT	OPTIONS				
INVOKED BY:	Menus		Commands		Other
FACILITIES	Help *	S/R Screens	Editors *	Debugging *	Other Utilities
INTERFACE TO:	DBMS *		TPM *		Other Software

PRICE/TERMS On application

INSTALLATIONS	NUMBER	FROM	TO
WORLD-WIDE			
IN UK			

DESCRIPTION: A relational DBMS designed for end-users, providing facilities for querying and manipulating data and writing reports. SQL statements, which are entered from a terminal or embedded in a program, perform such activities as updating and sorting data, making calculations on stored data and producing reports.

NAME SYSTEM BLDR5	VENDOR BCC

H/W DEC	OS	TPM	OTHER RMS COBOL

TYPE	TRANSLATOR		CODE GENERATOR				
	Compiler	Interpreter	Cobol	PL/1	Basic	Assembler	Other
			*				

EXECUTION MODE		OPERATION MODE	Batch	On-line	Multi-user
Under Product		Product	*	*	*
Independently	*	Application	*	*	*

SCOPE/ METHOD		DEFINITION OF:			
		Screens	Data	Processing	Reports
BY:	Screen Painting	*			*
	Form Filling		*		
	Questionnaire				
	Commands				

DEVELOPMENT ENVIRONMENT	OPTIONS				
INVOKED BY:	Menus *		Commands		Other
FACILITIES	Help *	S/R Screens	Editors	Debugging	Other Utilities
INTERFACE TO:	DBMS		TPM		Other Software *

PRICE/TERMS   From $12,000 to $35,000

INSTALLATIONS	NUMBER	FROM	TO
WORLD-WIDE	25		
IN UK			

DESCRIPTION: SB-5 is a comprehensive system for the automated design, production, documentation and maintenance of COBOL application systems for DEC hardware. Produces pre-compiled design specs, full user and programmer documentation, cross-referenced by field reports, project statistics report and program flow report.

NAME	SYSTEMMASTER	VENDOR	EDP

H/W Q1	OS	TPM	OTHER

TYPE	TRANSLATOR		CODE GENERATOR				
	Compiler	Interpreter	Cobol	PL/1	Basic	Assembler	Other
		*					

EXECUTION MODE			OPERATION MODE	Batch	On-line	Multi-user
Under Product	*		Product	*	*	
Independently			Application	*	*	*

SCOPE/ METHOD		DEFINITION OF:			
		Screens	Data	Processing	Reports
BY:	Screen Painting				
	Form Filling		*	*	*
	Questionnaire	*			
	Commands				

DEVELOPMENT ENVIRONMENT	OPTIONS				
INVOKED BY:	Menus *		Commands		Other *
FACILITIES	Help	S/R Screens	Editors *	Debugging *	Other Utilities
INTERFACE TO:	DBMS		TPM		Other Software *

PRICE/TERMS	To be announced

INSTALLATIONS	NUMBER	FROM	TO
WORLD-WIDE			
IN UK	1	1/09/82	31/12/82

DESCRIPTION: A system generator designed to permit rapid development of integrated systems for the smaller business user. The product is designed for the Q1 local area network computer.

NAME TAGS	VENDOR DATABASE

H/W PRIME	OS PRIMOS	TPM	OTHER

TYPE	TRANSLATOR		CODE GENERATOR				
	Compiler	Interpreter	Cobol	PL/1	Basic	Assembler	Other
	*	*					

EXECUTION MODE		OPERATION MODE	Batch	On-line	Multi-user
Under Product	*	Product		*	*
Independently		Application		*	*

SCOPE/ METHOD		DEFINITION OF:			
		Screens	Data	Processing	Reports
BY:	Screen Painting	*			
	Form Filling	*	*		
	Questionnaire				
	Commands			*	*

DEVELOPMENT ENVIRONMENT	OPTIONS				
INVOKED BY:	Menus *		Commands		Other
FACILITIES	Help	S/R Screens	Editors *	Debugging *	Other Utilities *
INTERFACE TO:	DBMS		TPM		Other Software *

PRICE/TERMS   From £8,500 (modular)

INSTALLATIONS	NUMBER	FROM	TO
WORLD-WIDE	150		31/12/82
IN UK	3	1/01/83	28/02/83

DESCRIPTION: Total Application Generating System (TAGS) integrates three application development tools:
TRANSACT – on-line transaction processor
FAST – multi-key file management system
FACTS – interactive data management and reporting system

NAME	TLO	VENDOR	DJAI

H/W	MICRO	OS	VARIOUS	TPM		OTHER	BASIC

TYPE	TRANSLATOR		CODE GENERATOR				
	Compiler	Interpreter	Cobol	PL/1	Basic	Assembler	Other
					*		

EXECUTION MODE			OPERATION MODE	Batch	On-line	Multi-user
Under Product			Product		*	
Independently	*		Application		*	

SCOPE/ METHOD		DEFINITION OF:			
		Screens	Data	Processing	Reports
BY:	Screen Painting				
	Form Filling				
	Questionnaire	*	*	*	*
	Commands				

DEVELOPMENT ENVIRONMENT	OPTIONS				
INVOKED BY:	Menus *		Commands		Other
FACILITIES	Help *	S/R Screens	Editors *	Debugging	Other Utilities
INTERFACE TO:	DBMS		TPM		Other Software *

PRICE/TERMS	£260

INSTALLATIONS	NUMBER	FROM	TO
WORLD-WIDE			
IN UK			

DESCRIPTION: A BASIC code generator for microcomputers. Widely used, but no precise sales figures available.

NAME TRANS IV	VENDOR INFORMATICS

H/W IBM	OS VSE VS1 MVS	TPM CICS	OTHER

	TRANSLATOR		CODE GENERATOR			
TYPE	Compiler	Interpreter	Cobol	PL/1	Basic	Assembler	Other
		*					

EXECUTION MODE		OPERATION MODE	Batch	On-line	Multi-user
Under Product	*	Product		*	
Independently		Application		*	

SCOPE/ METHOD		DEFINITION OF:			
		Screens	Data	Processing	Reports
BY:	Screen Painting				
	Form Filling	*	*		
	Questionnaire				
	Commands		*	*	

DEVELOPMENT ENVIRONMENT	OPTIONS				
INVOKED BY:	Menus *		Commands		Other
FACILITIES	Help	S/R Screens	Editors *	Debugging *	Other Utilities
INTERFACE TO:	DBMS *		TPM *		Other Software *

PRICE/TERMS   From $22,000 (US price)

INSTALLATIONS	NUMBER	FROM	TO
WORLD-WIDE	135	1/01/80	31/12/82
IN UK			

DESCRIPTION: An interactive application development system for the on-line development, testing and maintenance of CICS/VS applications. It employs a menu-driven, fill-in-the-blanks technique and requires minimal CICS expertise at the application development level.

NAME UFO	VENDOR FEE

H/W IBM	OS DOS OS	TPM CICS IMS/C	OTHER

TYPE	TRANSLATOR		CODE GENERATOR				
	Compiler	Interpreter	Cobol	PL/1	Basic	Assembler	Other
		*					

EXECUTION MODE		OPERATION MODE	Batch	On-line	Multi-user
Under Product	*	Product		*	*
Independently		Application		*	*

SCOPE/ METHOD		DEFINITION OF:			
		Screens	Data	Processing	Reports
BY:	Screen Painting	*			*
	Form Filling	*	*		*
	Questionnaire				
	Commands		*	*	

DEVELOPMENT ENVIRONMENT	OPTIONS				
INVOKED BY:	Menus *		Commands		Other
FACILITIES	Help *	S/R Screens	Editors *	Debugging *	Other Utilities *
INTERFACE TO:	DBMS *		TPM *		Other Software *

PRICE/TERMS From £16,000

INSTALLATIONS	NUMBER	FROM	TO
WORLD-WIDE	850		31/12/82
IN UK	100		31/12/82

DESCRIPTION: An application development system which can be used by DP and non-DP staff for all aspects of system development.

NAME USER-11	VENDOR PIONEER

H/W DEC	OS RSTS VMS	TPM	OTHER

TYPE	TRANSLATOR		CODE GENERATOR				
	Compiler	Interpreter	Cobol	PL/1	Basic	Assembler	Other
	*	*			*		

EXECUTION MODE		OPERATION MODE	Batch	On-line	Multi-user
Under Product	*	Product	*	*	*
Independently	*	Application	*	*	*

SCOPE/ METHOD		DEFINITION OF:			
		Screens	Data	Processing	Reports
BY:	Screen Painting				
	Form Filling				
	Questionnaire	*	*	*	*
	Commands				

DEVELOPMENT ENVIRONMENT	OPTIONS				
INVOKED BY:	Menus		Commands		Other
FACILITIES	Help *	S/R Screens	Editors *	Debugging *	Other Utilities *
INTERFACE TO:	DBMS		TPM		Other Software *

PRICE/TERMS From $12,000 (US price)

INSTALLATIONS	NUMBER	FROM	TO
WORLD-WIDE	180	1/01/78	31/12/82
IN UK	15	1/12/80	31/12/82

DESCRIPTION: Applications development system containing: central DD, file maintenance utilities, report generator, screen generator, data manipulation language, BASIC program generator and security system.

NAME USERTAB	VENDOR NCC

H/W PORTABLE	OS VARIOUS	TPM VARIOUS	OTHER

TYPE	TRANSLATOR		CODE GENERATOR				
	Compiler	Interpreter	Cobol	PL/1	Basic	Assembler	Other
							*

EXECUTION MODE		OPERATION MODE	Batch	On-line	Multi-user
Under Product		Product	*		
Independently	*	Application	*		

SCOPE/ METHOD		DEFINITION OF:			
		Screens	Data	Processing	Reports
BY:	Screen Painting				
	Form Filling				
	Questionnaire				
	Commands		*	*	*

DEVELOPMENT ENVIRONMENT	OPTIONS				
INVOKED BY:	Menus		Commands		Other
FACILITIES	Help	S/R Screens	Editors	Debugging	Other Utilities
INTERFACE TO:	DBMS		TPM		Other Software *

PRICE/TERMS	On application

INSTALLATIONS	NUMBER	FROM	TO
WORLD-WIDE			
IN UK	100	1/01/81	31/12/82

DESCRIPTION: Reporting and ad-hoc enquiry. Particularly aimed at non-DP users.

Appendix B

Comparison Tables

The following tables list the APG products against the various attributes described in the product summary details of Appendix A. For each product, the appropriate attributes are indicated by an asterisk in the relevant row, column position of the table.

Appendix B.1   Type of Product Comparison Table

PRODUCT NAME	TRANSLATOR		CODE GENERATOR					EXECUTES	
	Comp	Int	COBOL	PL/1	Assem	BASIC	Other	UP	Ind
ACT/1	*	*	*	*				*	
ADAM			*						*
ADF	*	*						*	
ADMINS/V32		*						*	
ADS/O	*							*	
ALL		*						*	
APPBUILD			*	*			*		*
AUTOCODE							*		*
CARS			*						*
CMS						*			*
COBMAN			*						*
COBOL/DL			*						*
CODE			*						*
COGEN			*						*
CPG	*				*			*	*
CUPID		*						*	
DATAPLAN						*			*
DELTA				*					*
ELIAS			*	*			*		*
FACTORY		*						*	
FILETAB		*						*	
FMS-80		*						*	
FOCUS		*						*	
GENERATION 5		*						*	
GRASS/34							*		*
GRS		*						*	
HLC			*						*
IDEAL	*	*						*	
INFO		*						*	
INSYST		*						*	
LINC	*		*					*	
MANTIS		*						*	
MAPPER		*						*	
MARK IV	*						*		*
MARK V	*						*		*
MIMER			*				*		*

Appendix B.1 (Cont)

PRODUCT NAME	TRANSLATOR		CODE GENERATOR					EXECUTES	
	Comp	Int	COBOL	PL/1	Assem	BASIC	Other	UP	Ind
MIS/OL			*	*					*
MM								*	
MUM		*						*	
NATURAL	*							*	
NUCLEUS						*			*
OLGEN	*		*						*
ORACLE (1)		*						*	
ORACLE (2)		*						*	
PACT			*	*					*
PANEL			*	*			*		*
PER PEARL		*						*	
PRELUDE						*		*	
PRIDE			*	*					*
PRO/GRAMMAR	*	*						*	
PROGAPP						*			*
PROMACS			*						*
RAMIS		*						*	
RAPID		*						*	
RDM		*						*	
READYCODE			*						*
SILICON OFF		*						*	
SOFTOOL							*		*
SQL/DS	*							*	
SYSTEM BLDR5			*						*
SYSTEMMASTER		*						*	
TAGS	*	*						*	
TLO						*			*
TRANS IV		*						*	
UFO		*						*	
USER-11	*	*				*		*	*
USERTAB							*		*

KEY: Comp – Compiler, Int – Interpreter, Assem – Assembler, UP – Under Product, Ind – Independently

Appendix B.2   Mode of Operation Comparison Table

PRODUCT NAME	PRODUCT			APPLICATION		
	On-line	Batch	Multi-user	On-line	Batch	Multi-user
ACT/1	*		*	*		
ADAM	*	*	*	*	*	*
ADF	*	*	*	*	*	*
ADMINS/V32	*		*	*		*
ADS/O	*	*	*	*	*	*
ALL	*		*	*	*	*
APPBUILD	*	*	*	*	*	*
AUTCODE	*			*		
CARS		*			*	
CMS	*		*	*		*
COBMAN	*	*		*	*	*
COBOL/DL	*	*		*	*	
CODE	*	*		*	*	*
COGEN						
CPG	*			*	*	
CUPID	*		*	*	*	*
DATAPLAN	*		*	*		*
DELTA	*	*	*	*	*	*
ELIAS	*			*	*	
FACTORY	*		*	*		*
FILETAB		*			*	
FMS-80	*		*	*		*
FOCUS	*	*	*	*	*	*
GENERATION5						
GRASS/34	*		*	*		*
GRS	*	*	*	*	*	*
HLC	*	*	*	*	*	*
IDEAL	*		*	*	*	*
INFO	*		*	*	*	*
INSYST	*		*	*		*
LINC	*	*	*	*	*	*
MANTIS	*		*	*		*
MAPPER	*		*	*		*
MARK IV		*	*		*	*
MARK V	*	*	*	*		*

Appendix B.2 (Cont)

PRODUCT NAME	PRODUCT			APPLICATION		
	On-line	Batch	Multi-user	On-line	Batch	Multi-user
MIMER	*		*	*		*
MIS/OL	*		*	*		*
MM	*		*	*		*
MUM	*		*	*		*
NATURAL	*	*	*	*	*	*
NUCLEUS	*			*		
OLGEN	*		*	*		*
ORACLE (1)	*		*	*		*
ORACLE (2)	*		*	*		*
PACT	*	*			*	
PANEL	*			*		
PER PEARL	*			*		
PRELUDE	*		*	*		*
PRIDE	*		*	*	*	*
PRO/GRAMMAR		*			*	*
PROGAPP	*			*		
PROMACS	*			*	*	*
RAMIS	*	*		*	*	
RAPID	*		*	*		*
RDM	*		*	*		*
READYCODE	*	*	*	*	*	*
SILICON OFF	*			*		
SOFTOOL	*		*	*		*
SQL/DS	*	*	*	*	*	*
SYSTEM BLDR5	*	*	*	*	*	*
SYSTEMMASTER	*	*		*	*	*
TAGS	*		*	*		*
TLO	*			*		
TRANS IV	*			*		
UFO	*		*	*		*
USER-11	*	*	*	*	*	*
USERTAB		*			*	

Appendix B.3   Scope/Method Comparison Table

PRODUCT NAME	SCREENS				DATA				PROCESSING				REPORTS			
	SP	FF	Q	C	SP	FF	Q	C	SP	FF	Q	C	SP	FF	Q	C
ACT/1	*															
ADAM				*				*				*				*
ADF				*				*				*				
ADMINS/V32		*				*						*		*		
ADS/O	*											*				
ALL			*				*					*			*	
APPBUILD		*				*						*		*		
AUTOCODE		*				*								*		
CARS								*				*				*
CMS			*			*						*		*		
COBMAN				*				*								*
COBOL/DL								*				*				*
CODE				*				*				*				*
COGEN																
CPG	*					*						*				*
CUPID		*				*				*				*		
DATAPLAN				*				*				*				*
DELTA				*				*				*				*
ELIAS		*				*										
FACTORY			*				*					*			*	
FILETAB								*				*				*
FMS-80	*	*			*	*						*		*		
FOCUS		*	*	*		*	*	*		*	*	*		*	*	*
GENERATION 5																
GRASS/34			*				*								*	
GRS												*				*
HLC				*				*				*				*
IDEAL	*	*				*						*	*	*		
INFO	*							*				*	*			
INSYST		*				*				*						
LINC	*					*						*	*			
MANTIS	*			*		*						*	*			
MAPPER				*				*				*				*
MARK IV						*		*		*		*		*		*

Appendix B.3 (Cont)

PRODUCT NAME	SCREENS SP	FF	Q	C	DATA SP	FF	Q	C	PROCESSING SP	FF	Q	C	REPORTS SP	FF	Q	C
MARK V	*			*				*			*					
MIMER				*				*			*					*
MIS/OL	*					*										
MM		*														
MUM		*				*				*				*		
NATURAL		*				*					*			*		
NUCLEUS			*				*				*				*	
OLGEN		*				*	*							*	*	
ORACLE (1)	*	*						*			*					
ORACLE (2)	*			*				*			*					*
PACT								*								*
PANEL	*					*										
PER PEARL	*					*							*			
PRELUDE	*							*			*		*			
PRIDE			*				*				*				*	
PRO/GRAMMAR								*			*					*
PROGAPP	*					*					*		*			
PROMACS				*				*			*					*
RAMIS	*	*		*	*	*		*			*					*
RAPID		*				*					*					*
RDM																
READYCODE	*	*				*							*	*		
SILICON OFF				*				*			*					*
SOFTOOL																
SQL/DS								*			*					*
SYSTEM BLDR5	*					*							*			
SYSTEMMASTER			*			*				*				*		
TAGS	*	*				*					*					*
TLO			*				*				*				*	
TRANS IV		*				*		*			*					
UFO	*	*				*		*			*		*	*		
USER-11			*				*				*				*	
USERTAB								*			*					*

KEY: SP – Screen Painting, FF – Form Filling, Q – Questionnaire, C – Commands

Appendix B.4   Development Environment (1) Comparison Table

PRODUCT NAME	METHOD OF INVOKING			SPECIAL FEATURES	
	Menus	Commands	Other	Help	S/R Screens
ACT/1	*			*	*
ADAM	*				
ADF					
ADMINS/V32			*		
ADS/O	*			*	
ALL	*			*	
APPBUILD	*			*	
AUTOCODE	*				
CARS					
CMS	*			*	
COBMAN					
COBOL/DL	*			*	
CODE					
COGEN					
CPG	*			*	
CUPID					
DATAPLAN					
DELTA					
ELIAS	*			*	
FACTORY					
FILETAB					
FMS-80	*			*	*
FOCUS			*	*	
GENERATION5					
GRASS/34	*				
GRS					
HLC					
IDEAL	*		*	*	*
INFO	*			*	
INSYST			*		
LINC					
MANTIS	*			*	
MAPPER				*	
MARK IV					

Appendix B.4 (Cont)

PRODUCT NAME	METHOD OF INVOKING			SPECIAL FEATURES	
	Menus	Commands	Other	Help	S/R Screens
MARK V			*		*
MIMER					
MIS/OL					
MM					
MUM	*		*		
NATURAL				*	
NUCLEUS	*				
OLGEN	*			*	
ORACLE (1)	*				
ORACLE (2)	*			*	
PACT					
PANEL					
PER PEARL	*			*	
PRELUDE	*				
PRIDE	*			*	
PRO/GRAMMAR					
PROGAPP	*			*	
PROMACS					
RAMIS				*	
RAPID	*			*	
RDM					
READYCODE	*		*	*	
SILICON OFF	*			*	
SOFTOOL					
SQL/DS				*	
SYSTEM BLDR5	*			*	
SYSTEMMASTER	*		*		
TAGS	*				
TLO	*			*	
TRANS IV	*				
UFO	*			*	
USER-11				*	
USERTAB					

Appendix B.5 Development Environment (2) Comparison Table

PRODUCT NAME	FACILITIES			TRANSPARENT INTERFACE TO		
	Editors	Debugging	Other U	DBMS	TPM	Other S/W
ACT/1	*	*			*	*
ADAM				*	*	*
ADF				*	*	
ADMINS/V32						*
ADS/O	*	*	*	*	*	*
ALL	*	*	*			*
APPBUILD	*	*		*	*	*
AUTOCODE						*
CARS						
CMS						*
COBMAN				*	*	*
COBOL/DL				*	*	*
CODE						
COGEN						
CPG	*	*		*	*	*
CUPID	*					
DATAPLAN						
DELTA						*
ELIAS	*			*	*	*
FACTORY						*
FILETAB					*	*
FMS-80	*	*	*			*
FOCUS	*	*	*	*	*	*
GENERATION5						
GRASS/34						
GRS						*
HLC						
IDEAL	*	*	*	*	*	*
INFO	*	*		*	*	*
INSYST						
LINC	*	*	*	*	*	*
MANTIS	*	*	*	*	*	*
MAPPER	*	*	*	*	*	
MARK IV	*	*	*	*	*	*

Appendix B.5 (Cont)

PRODUCT NAME	FACILITIES			TRANSPARENT INTERFACE TO		
	Editors	Debugging	Other U	DBMS	TPM	Other S/W
MARK V	*	*	*	*	*	*
MIMER						
MIS/OL			*	*	*	*
MM	*	*		*	*	*
MUM	*					*
NATURAL	*	*	*	*	*	
NUCLEUS				.		*
OLGEN	*					
ORACLE (1)					*	*
ORACLE (2)	*	*		*	*	*
PACT						
PANEL						*
PER PEARL	*					
PRELUDE						
PRIDE	*					
PRO/GRAMMAR				*		*
PROGAPP	*	*				
PROMACS				*	*	*
RAMIS	*	*	*	*	*	*
RAPID	*	*	*			*
RDM						
READYCODE	*	*	*	*	*	*
SILICON OFF	*	*	*			*
SOFTOOL						
SQL/DS	*	*		*	*	
SYSTEM BLDR5						*
SYSTEMMASTER	*	*				*
TAGS	*	*	*			*
TLO	*					*
TRANS IV	*	*		*	*	*
UFO	*	*	*	*	*	*
USER-11	*	*	*			*
USER TAB						*

KEY: Other U – Other Utilities, Other S/W – Other Software

Appendix C

Cross-reference Tables

This appendix consists of Product/Vendor and Vendor/Product cross-reference tables. The required hardware category is also included in the tables.

Appendix C.1

Product/Vendor Cross-reference Table

PRODUCT NAME	HARDWARE	VENDOR
ACT/1	IBM	WESTINGHOUSE
ADAM	IBM	CACI
ADF	IBM	IBM
ADMINS/V32	DEC VAX	CELERITY
ADS/O	IBM	CULLINANE
ALL	CMC	CMC
APPBUILD	IBM DEC NIXDORF	DMW
AUTOCODE	MICRO	STEMMOS
CARS	PORTABLE	SAGE
CMS	DATA GENERAL	CML
COBMAN	ICL, ATLAS, IBM	COBRA
COBOL/DL	IBM	ADR
CODE	IBM	SHUBROOKS
COGEN	NCR	RX
CPG	IBM	ALTERGO
CUPID	DEC	TUBS
DATAPLAN	DATA GENERAL	CSS
DELTA	PORTABLE	DELTA
ELIAS	IBM	IBM
FACTORY	DEC VAX	CORTEX
FILETAB	PORTABLE	NCC
FMS-80	MICRO	INFODATA
FOCUS	IBM	INFOBUILD
GENERATION 5	IBM	DATASOLVE
GRASS/34	IBM SYSTEM 34	PRESTEDGE
GRS	DEC	SYSCOM
HLC	MAINFRAME	S+PC
IDEAL	IBM	ADR
INFO	PORTABLE	DORIC
INSYST	IBM	CIRCLE
LINC	B1000-7000	BURROUGHS
MANTIS	IBM	CINCOM
MAPPER	UNIVAC	SPERRY

PRODUCT NAME	HARDWARE	VENDOR
MARK IV	IBM 370	INFORMATICS
MARK V	IBM 370	INFORMATICS
MIMER	PORTABLE	SAVANT
MIS/OL	IBM	PANSOPHIC
MM	IBM	TSI
MUM	MINI	FRETWELL
NATURAL	IBM	ADABAS
NUCLEUS	MICRO	COMPACT
OLGEN	BURROUGHS	WATSONS
ORACLE (1)	ICL	DATAB
ORACLE (2)	DEC	CACI
PACT	IBM	THREE-D
PANEL	MICRO	ROUNDHILL
PER PEARL	MICRO	PEARL
PRELUDE	MINIS	CORES
PRIDE	PORTABLE	MBA
PRO/GRAMMAR	IBM	PANSOPHIC
PROGAPP	MICRO	LIFEBOAT
PROMACS	IBM	MACS
RAMIS	IBM	MATHEMATICA
RAPID	HP 3000	HP
RDM	DEC PDP-11	UNIT-C
READYCODE	IBM	DATA LOGIC
SILICON OFF	MICROS	BSF
SOFTOOL	VARIOUS	SOFTOOL
SQL/DS	IBM	IBM
SYSTEM BLDR5	DEC	BCC
SYSTEMMASTER	Q1	EDP
TAGS	PRIME	DATABASE
TLO	MICRO	DJAI
TRANS IV	IBM	INFORMATICS
UFO	IBM	FEE
USER-11	DEC	PIONEER
USERTAB	PORTABLE	NCC

Appendix C.2

Vendor/Product Cross-reference Table

VENDOR	HARDWARE	PRODUCT NAME
ADABAS	IBM	NATURAL
ADR	IBM	COBOL/DL
ADR	IBM	IDEAL
ALTERGO	IBM	CPG
BCC	DEC	SYSTEM BLDR5
BSF	MICROS	SILICON OFF
BURROUGHS	B1000-7000	LINC
CACI	DEC	ORACLE (2)
CACI	IBM	ADAM
CELERITY	DEC VAX	ADMINS/V32
CINCOM	IBM	MANTIS
CIRCLE	IBM	INSYST
CMC	CMC	ALL
CML	DATA GENERAL	CMS
COBRA	ICL, ATLAS, IBM	COBMAN
COMPACT	MICRO	NUCLEUS
CORES	MINIS	PRELUDE
CORTEX	DEC VAX	FACTORY
CSS	DATA GENERAL	DATAPLAN
CULLINANE	IBM	ADS/O
DATA LOGIC	IBM	READYCODE
DATAB	ICL	ORACLE (1)
DATABASE	PRIME	TAGS
DATASOLVE	IBM	GENERATION 5
DELTA	PORTABLE	DELTA
DJAI	MICRO	TLO
DMW	IBM DEC NIXDORF	APPBUILD
DORIC	PORTABLE	INFO
EDP	Q1	SYSTEMMASTER
FEE	IBM	UFO
FRETWELL	MINI	MUM
HP	HP 3000	RAPID
IBM	IBM	ADF

VENDOR	HARDWARE	PRODUCT NAME
IBM	IBM	ELIAS
IBM	IBM	SQL/DS
INFOBUILD	IBM	FOCUS
INFODATA	MICRO	FMS-80
INFORMATICS	IBM	TRANS IV
INFORMATICS	IBM 370	MARK IV
INFORMATICS	IBM 370	MARK V
LIFEBOAT	MICRO	PROGAPP
MACS	IBM	PROMACS
MATHEMATICA	IBM	RAMIS
MBA	PORTABLE	PRIDE
NCC	PORTABLE	FILETAB
NCC	PORTABLE	USERTAB
PANSOPHIC	IBM	MIS/OL
PANSOPHIC	IBM	PRO/GRAMMAR
PEARL	MICRO	PER PEARL
PIONEER	DEC	USER-11
PRESTEDGE	IBM SYSTEM 34	GRASS/34
ROUNDHILL	MICRO	PANEL
RX	NCR	COGEN
S+PC	MAINFRAME	HLC
SAGE	PORTABLE	CARS
SAVANT	PORTABLE	MIMER
SHUBROOKS	IBM	CODE
SOFTOOL	VARIOUS	SOFTOOL
SPERRY	UNIVAC	MAPPER
STEMMOS	MICRO	AUTOCODE
SYSCOM	DEC	GRS
THREE-D	IBM	PACT
TSI	IBM	MM
TUBS	DEC	CUPID
UNIT-C	DEC PDP-11	RDM
WATSONS	BURROUGHS	OLGEN
WESTINGHOUSE	IBM	ACT/1

Appendix D

Vendor Details

This appendix contains an alphabetical listing of vendors. Information about vendor names, addresses and telephone numbers is given, together with the relevant product name(s).

VENDOR	VENDOR DETAILS	PRODUCT
ADABAS	ADABAS SOFTWARE LIMITED Laurie House 22 Colyear Street DERBY DE1 1LA Tel: 0332 372535 SOFTWARE AG Hilpertstrasse 20 8100 DARMSTADT West Germany Tel: 06151 82747	NATURAL
ADR	APPLIED DATA RESEARCH LIMITED Portmill House 37-40 Portmill Lane HITCHIN, Hertfordshire SG5 1DJ Tel: 0462 55353 APPLIED DATA RESEARCH INCORPORATED Route 206, Orchard Road CN-8 PRINCETON New Jersey, USA NJ 08540 Tel: 201 874 9000	1) COBOL/DL 2) IDEAL
ALTERGO	ALTERGO SOFTWARE LIMITED Ringwood House Walton Street, AYLESBURY, Buckinghamshire Tel: 0296 32011	CPG
BCC	BUSINESS CONTROLS CORPORATION 507 Boulevard ELMWOOD PARK New Jersey, USA NJ 07407	SYSTEM BLDR5
BSF	THE BRISTOL SOFTWARE FACTORY Kingsons House Grove Avenue, Queen Square BRISTOL BS1 4QY	SILICON OFF

VENDOR	VENDOR DETAILS	PRODUCT
BURROUGHS	BURROUGHS MACHINES LIMITED Heathrow House Bath Road HOUNSLOW, Middlesex Tel: 01 750 1400	LINC
CACI	CACI INC INTERNATIONAL Swan Office Centre 1506-1508 Coventry Road Yardley, BIRMINGHAM B25 8AD Tel: 021 706 8103	1) ADAM 2) ORACLE (2)
CELERITY	CELERITY SOFTWARE LIMITED PO Box 122 HEMEL HEMPSTEAD, Hertfordshire HP1 1RA Tel: 0442 62659 ADMINS INC PO Box 269 CAMBRIDGE Massachusetts, USA MA 02138 Tel: 617 661 3206	ADMINS/V32
CINCOM	CINCOM SYSTEMS (UK) LIMITED St. Ives House St. Ives Road MAIDENHEAD, Berkshire Tel; 0628 72731/847198 CINCOM SYSTEMS INC 2300 Montana Avenue CINCINNATI Ohio, USA OH 45211 Tel: 513 662 2300	MANTIS
CIRCLE	CIRCLE COMPUTER CONSULTANTS LIMITED 15 High Street Chalfont St. Peter GERRARDS CROSS, Buckinghamshire SL9 9QE	INSYST

VENDOR	VENDOR DETAILS	PRODUCT
CMC	CMC INTERNATIONAL LIMITED Maylands House Maylands Avenue HEMEL HEMPSTEAD, Hertfordshire Tel: 0442 61266	ALL
CML	COMPUTER MODELLING LIMITED Oak House Manor Road PENN, Buckinghamshire HP10 8HY Tel: 049 481 6181	CMS
COBRA	COBRA SYSTEMS & PROGRAMMING LIMITED 21 Green Hill Road CAMBERLEY, Surrey GU15 1PF Tel: 0276 25163	COBMAN
COMPACT	COMPACT ACCOUNTING SERVICES LIMITED Cape House Cape Place DORKING, Surrey	NUCLEUS
CORES	CORES LIMITED & UNIVERSAL COMPUTERS LIMITED 23 Paradise Street LONDON SE16 4QD	PRELUDE
CORTEX	CORTEX CORPORATION 55 William Street WELLESLEY Massachusetts, USA MA 02181 Tel: 617 237 2304	FACTORY
CSS	COMPUTERPLAN SOFTWARE SERVICES LIMITED Business Equipment 502 Kingsland Road LONDON E8 4AE Tel: 01 254 1674	DATAPLAN

VENDOR	VENDOR DETAILS	PRODUCT
CULLINANE	CULLINANE (UK) LIMITED Premier House 150 Southampton Row LONDON WC1B 5AL Tel: 01 837 9616 CULLINANE DATABASE SYSTEMS INC 400 Blue Hill Drive WESTWOOD Massachusetts, USA MA 02090 Tel: 617 329 7700	ADS/O
DATA LOGIC	DATA LOGIC LIMITED (READYCODE DEVELOPMENT SERVICES) Data Logic House Bradfield Close WOKING, Surrey GU22 7RF Tel: 04862 71971 RAYTHEON COMPUTER SERVICES 195 Worcester Road WELLESLEY Massachusetts, USA MA 02181	READYCODE
DATAB	DATAB (UK) LIMITED Oak House Manor Road PENN, Buckinghamshire	ORACLE (1)
DATABASE	DATABASE SYSTEMS LIMITED Gainsborough House 15 High Street HARPENDEN, Hertfordshire AL5 4RT DATABASE SYSTEMS CORP 1846 East Camelback Road, Suite 200 PHOENIX Arizona, USA AZ 85016	TAGS
DATASOLVE	AMERICAN MANAGEMENT SYSTEMS LIMITED 1777 North Kent Street ARLINGTON Virginia, USA VA 22209	GENERATION 5

VENDOR	VENDOR DETAILS	PRODUCT
DELTA	DELTA SOFTWARE TOOLS LIMITED 46 Kingsway LONDON WC2B 6EN Tel: 01 405 4844 SODECON AG Bahnhofplatz 26 CH-8603 SCHWERZENBACH Switzerland	DELTA
DJAI	DJAI SYSTEMS LIMITED Station Road ILMINSTER, Somerset TA19 9BQ Tel: 04605 4117	TLO
DMW	THE DMW GROUP Spa House 11/17 Worple Road Wimbledon, LONDON SW19 4JS Tel: 01 946 9109	APPBUILD
DORIC	DORIC COMPUTER SYSTEMS 25 Woodford Road WATFORD, Hertfordshire WD1 1PB Tel: 0923 52288 HENCO SOFTWARE INC 100 Fifth Avenue WALTHAM Massachusetts, USA MA 02154 Tel: 617 890 8670	INFO
EDP	EUROPA DATA PRODUCTS (UK) LIMITED Langley House Stanneylands Road WILMSLOW, Cheshire Tel: Wilmslow 532127	SYSTEMMASTER

VENDOR	VENDOR DETAILS	PRODUCT
FEE	FEE LIMITED Priorty House California Lane Bushey Heath, WATFORD, Hertfordshire WORLDWIDE SOFTWARE ASSOCIATES INC 174 Boulevard HASBROUCK HEIGHTS New Jersey, USA	UFO
FRETWELL	F. FRETWELL-DOWNING LIMITED 5 Onslow Road SHEFFIELD S11 7AE Tel: 0742 682301	MUM
HP	HEWLETT-PACKARD Inquiry Department King Street Lane Winnersh WOKINGHAM, Berkshire RG11 1BR or contact the local office	RAPID
IBM	INTERNATIONAL BUSINESS MACHINES CORPORATION Data Processing Division 1133 Westchester Avenue WHITE PLAINS New York, USA NY 10604 or contact the local office	1) ADF 2) ELIAS 3) SQL/DS
INFOBUILD	INFORMATION BUILDERS (UK) LIMITED Fifth Floor, Station House Harrow Road WEMBLEY HA9 6DE Tel: 01 903 6111 INFORMATION BUILDERS INC 1250 Broadway NEW YORK New York, USA Tel: 212 736 4433	FOCUS

VENDOR	VENDOR DETAILS	PRODUCT
INFODATA	INFODATA SYSTEMS LIMITED Chaucer Estate Easton Lane WINCHESTER, Hampshire SO23 7RU Tel: 0962 60744 DJR ASSOCIATES INC 303 South Broadway TARRYTOWN New York, USA NY 10591 Tel: 914 631 6766	FMS-80
INFORMATICS	INFORMATICS (UK) LIMITED Ground Floor, Africa House 64-78 Kingsway LONDON WC2B 6AL Tel: 01 831 6751 INFORMATICS GENERAL CORPORATION 21050 Vanowen Street CANOGA PARK California, USA CA 91304 Tel: 213 716 1616	1) MARK IV 2) MARK V 3) TRANS IV
LIFEBOAT	LIFEBOAT ASSOCIATES PO Box 125 LONDON WC2H 9LU Tel: 01 836 9028 LIFEBOAT ASSOCIATES 1651 Third Avenue NEW YORK New York, USA NY 10028	PROGAPP
MACS	MANAGEMENT & COMPUTER SERVICES INC Great Valley Corporate Centre VALLEY FORGE Pennsylvania, USA PA 19482 Tel: 215 648 7030	PROMACS

VENDOR	VENDOR DETAILS	PRODUCT
MATHEMATICA	MATHEMATICA PRODUCTS GROUP 79-83 Great Portland Street LONDON W1N 5RA Tel: 01 580 3681 MATHEMATICA PRODUCTS GROUP INC PO 2392 PRINCETON New Jersey, USA NJ 08540	RAMIS
MBA	HOLLAND INTERNATIONAL COMPUTER SERVICES HOLDING BV Laan Van Meerdervoort 92 DEN HAIG 2517 AP The Netherlands	PRIDE
NCC	NATIONAL COMPUTING CENTRE LIMITED Oxford Road MANCHESTER M1 7ED Tel: 061 228 6333	1) FILETAB 2) USERTAB
PANSOPHIC	PANSOPHIC SYSTEMS (UK) LIMITED Achilles House Western Avenue Acton, LONDON W3 QUA Tel: 01 993 5985 PANSOPHIC SYSTEMS INC 709 Enterprise Drive OAK BROOK Illinois, USA IL 60521 Tel: 312 986 6000	1) MIS/OL 2) PRO/ GRAMMAR
PEARL	PEARL INTERNATIONAL Audley Lodge 15 Glenair Road POOLE, Dorset Tel: 0202 741 275	PER PEARL
PIONEER	PIONEER COMPUTER SYSTEMS LIMITED 4 Albion Place NORTHAMPTON NN1 1UD	USER-11

VENDOR	VENDOR DETAILS	PRODUCT
PRESTEDGE	PRESTEDGE CONSULTANTS LIMITED 3 Cecil Square MARGATE, Kent CT9 1BD	GRASS/34
ROUNDHILL	ROUNDHILL COMPUTER SYSTEMS LIMITED PO Box 14 MARLBOROUGH, Wiltshire SN8 1LG	PANEL
RX	RX COMPUTER LIMITED Cardale Grange Beckwithshaw, HARROGATE HG3 1QL Tel: 0423 51076 SOFTWARE CLEARING HOUSE 771 Neeb Road CINCINNATI Ohio, USA OH 45238	COGEN
S+PC	S+PC SYSTEMS LIMITED 69 Merton Hall Road Wimbledon, LONDON SW19 3PX	HLC
SAGE	SAGE SYSTEMS INC Audit Systems Division 5161 River Road BETHESDA Maryland, USA MY 20816 Tel: 301 986 1333	CARS
SAVANT	SAVANT 2 New Street CARNFORTH, Lancashire LA5 9BX Tel: 0524 734505 UPPSALA UNIVERSITY DATA CENTRA Box 2103 S-750 02 UPPSALA Sweden	MIMER
SHUBROOKS	SHUBROOKS Almners Priory Almners Road LYNE, Near Chertsey, Surrey Tel: 09328 66812	CODE

VENDOR	VENDOR DETAILS	PRODUCT
SOFTOOL	SOFTOOL CORPORATION 340 South Kellog Avenue GOLETA California, USA CA 93117	SOFTOOL
SPERRY	SPERRY Lynnfield House Church Street ALTRINCHAM, Cheshire Tel: 061 928 6400 SPERRY Software Development Centre 2276 Highcrest Drive ROSEVILLE Minnesoata, USA MI 55113	MAPPER
STEMMOS	STEMMOS LIMITED 344 Kensington High Street LONDON W14 Tel: 01 602 6242	AUTO CODE
SYSCOM	SYSCOM COMPUTERS LIMITED Kelvin House The Broadway DUDLEY, West Midlands DY1 4PY	GRS
THREE-D	3D SYSTEMS 27 Shenley Hill RADLETT, Hertfordshire WD7 7AU Tel: 09276 4435	PACT
TSI	TSI International Limited Park House 22 Park Street CROYDON, Surrey CR0 1YE	MM

VENDOR	VENDOR DETAILS	PRODUCT
TUBS	TUBS SOFTWARE LIMITED 30 New Walk LEICESTER LE1 6TW Tel: 0533 551410 TUBS SOFTWARE INC 654 Bair Island Road No 302 REDWOOD CITY California, USA CA 94063	CUPID
UNIT-C	UNIT-C Dominion Way West Broadwater WORTHING, Sussex BN14 8NT	RDM
WATSONS	WATSONS COMPUTERS SERVICES LIMITED Brasenose Road Bootle, LIVERPOOL L20 8HP Tel: 051 933 7027 ESI 11801 South Gadsden Street TALLAHASSEE Florida. USA FL 32301	OLGEN
WESTINGHOUSE	WESTINGHOUSE 1 High Street EDGEWARE, Middlesex HA8 7DF	ACT/1

Appendix E

Bibliography

This appendix contains an alphabetical list of books, papers and articles used in the preparation of this book.

Advanced Systems Development Techniques, 179540 in The Diebold Research Programme – Software and Methodology Series, Diebold Group Inc, October 1979.

Application Development Without Programmers, James Martin, Savant Institute Research Studies, 1981.

Application Generators – Implications For The Future, David Broughton, *BIS conference paper,* 1982.

Automated Software Development Elimates Application Programming, R Colin Johnson, *Electronics,* June 1982.

Data Management Systems, *EDP Analyser,* May 1981.

Data Processing in 1980-1985 – A Study of Potential Limitations to Progress, T A Dolotta et al, Wiley, 1976.

Developing Systems by Prototyping, *EDP Analyser,* September 1981.

Expert Systems – A Key Innovation in Professional and Managerial Problem Solving, Paul Ellis, *Information Age,* January 1983.

Fourth Generation Languages Evaluation, David Whiteside, *BIS conference paper,* 1982.

Future Processing – State of the Art Report, Infotech International, 1978.

Generators Do The Trick, Jan Synders, *Computer Decision,* June 1982.

History of Manchester Computers, S H Lavington, NCC Publications, 1975.

On-line Application Generators, *Xephon Buyers Guide,* 1983.

Programming by End Users, *EDP Analyser,* June 1981.

Programming Languages, James W Hunt, *Computer,* 1982.

Software Concepts in Process Control, R Alan Chard, NCC Publications, 1983.

Software Design, Judith C Erhos and R L Von Tilbury, *Computer,* February 1981.

The Cost Effectiveness of Systems Development Aids, Diebold Research Programme, Diebold Group Inc, 1981.

The Future of Programming, Anthony I Wasserman and Steven Goetz, *Communications of the ACM,* March 1982.

Index

169